The 'Hellenization' of Judaea in the
First Century after Christ

MARTIN HENGEL

The 'Hellenization' of Judaea in the First Century after Christ

in collaboration with
Christoph Markschies

SCM PRESS
London

TRINITY PRESS INTERNATIONAL
Philadelphia

Translated by John Bowden from the German 'Zum Problem der "Hellenisierung" Judäas im 1. Jahrhundert nach Christus'

© Martin Hengel 1989

Translation © John Bowden 1989

First published 1989

SCM Press Ltd
26-30 Tottenham Road
London N1 4BZ

Trinity Press International
3725 Chestnut Street
Philadelphia, Pa. 19104

British Library Cataloguing in Publication Data

Hengel, Martin
    The 'Hellenization' of Judaea in the first century after Christ.
    1. Judaism, History
    I. Title   II. Markschies, Christoph   II. Problem der Hellenisierung Judäas im 1. Jahrhundert nach Christus.
    English
    296'.09

    ISBN 0-334-00602-3

Library of Congress Cataloging-in-Publication Data

Hengel, Martin.
    [Zum Problem der "Hellenisierung" Judäas im 1. Jahrhundert nach Christus. English]
    The 'Hellenization" of Judaea in the first century after Christ / Martin Hengel.
        p.   cm.
    ISBN 0-334-00602-3
    1. Judaism—Relations—Greek. 2. Hellenism. 3. Jews--Civilization—Greek influences. 4. Judaism—History—Post-exilic period, 586 B.C.–210 A.D.   I. Title.
    BM536.G7H4713   1989
    296'.0933—dc20   89-20469

Phototypeset by Input Typesetting Ltd, London
and printed in Great Britain by
Richard Clay Ltd, Bungay, Suffolk

VENERANDO ORDINI THEOLOGORUM
UNIVERSITATIS ARGENTORATIS
MAGNO THEOLOGIAE DOCTORIS HONORE ORNATUS
HUNC LIBELLUM
GRATO ANIMO
DEDICAT
AUCTOR

Contents

1

The Problem[1]

Ever since the beginning of critical investigation of the New Testament
in terms of the history of religion it has been customary to distinguish
between 'Judaism' and 'Hellenism' (or between 'Jewish' and 'Hellenistic') as two completely different entities, to some degree capable
of exact definition. Fundamental importance is often attached to this
distinction, in which case it then appears as one of the most important
criteria for historical interpretation in New Testament studies.[2] Here
'Hellenism' (and the adjective formed from it) as it is now understood
is a relatively recent term; the great scholar Droysen was the first to
attach its present significance to it about 150 years ago in connection
with II Macc.4.13 (see n.19 below). It is used in history and the study
of antiquity to describe that new civilization furthered above all by
the expedition of Alexander the Great and the Graeco-Macedonian
'colonial rule' which followed, a civilization which was shaped by the
gradual spread of the Greek language and of Greek forms of life and
thought. This very complex process continued under Roman rule in
the east of the Empire until the fourth century CE. In Syria, including
Cilicia, Commagene, northern Mesopotamia, Phoenicia, Judaea-
Palestine and Nabataean Arabia, this development only really came
to a climax in the Roman period.[3] In the Christian period there was
then a reversal and a new penetration of the 'eastern' languages
spoken by the Christianized rural population, for example Syriac and
Coptic. Because of its multiplicity and complexity the process cannot
be described by a single term in the religious sphere, for example by
the term 'syncretism' which is so popular a watchword among
Protestant theologians.[4] However, right up to the present day New
Testament scholarship has hardly been bothered by such complexity
and scholars have often used this term without reflecting on it very
much. Concepts, traditions, whole narratives, forms of thought and
literature are examined to see whether they are of a 'Jewish' or

'Hellenistic' origin and stamp, and attempts are made to draw conclusions from the findings.[5]

A scientific understanding of earliest Christianity, its history, its theological thought, and with it the 'historical-critical' interpretation of the New Testament now seems hardly conceivable without this distinction which we have come to take for granted – perhaps all too much for granted. The concern to attach clear labels has often given rise to polemical arguments, and still does so. We evidently cannot escape them any more than our fathers did. Scholars are still concerned yet again, and sometimes even agitated, as to whether individual concepts, complexes of ideas or even particular theologians of earliest Christianity like Paul, John or the author of Hebrews are to be understood in terms of 'Old Testament/Jewish tradition' or 'Hellenistic syncretism', 'Jewish apocalyptic' or 'Hellenistic Gnosticism' (or 'enthusiasm'), 'rabbinic legal thought' or 'Hellenistic mysticism'.[6] The fact that here a preference for the predicate 'Old Testament/Jewish' often goes with a more 'conservative' approach and a preference for all that is 'Hellenistic' goes with a more 'liberal' or 'critical' attitude has not helped to produce an objective discussion. All too often one gets the impression that such a great and impressive label is simply meant to conceal a lack of historical understanding.[7]

Nevertheless, there was often an awareness that this distinction was vague and relative, indeed in some circumstances even questionable, and therefore attempts were made at a more precise differentiation. For it was recognized that the greatest influence on the rise of the church did not really come from a contrast between 'Judaism' and 'Hellenism' but from a synthesis of the two forces, as for example in the 'Hellenistic Judaism' of the Diaspora of the Roman Empire. Now, however, as a rule this 'Hellenistic Judaism' became similarly detached more or less clearly from the Judaism of the Palestine mother country, from which in fact earliest Christianity had also emerged. This merely shifted the focal point of the question. A consequence of this differentiation was that the earlier, all too crude, distinction between the (Jewish Christian) Palestinian 'primitive community' and the (Gentile Christian) 'Hellenistic community', which goes back to Heitmüller and was still used by Bultmann, was supplemented by the important intermediary link of a 'Jewish Christian Hellenistic community'.[8] According to this pattern, which is popular today, first there was the earliest Palestinian community, either in Galilee or Jerusalem, which was followed by 'Jewish Christian Hellenistic' communities in Syria, for example in Damascus, where Paul became a Christian, but above all in Antioch, and finally by the predominantly 'Gentile Christian Hellenistic communities', principally in Asia Minor and in Greece, i.e. in the sphere entered by the Pauline mission. Here the contribution of the individual communities to the rise of primitive Christianity, its worship and its theological traditions is again disputed.[9]

In this connection the 'Hellenistic' Christianity of Syria enjoyed a special popularity; the decisive developments and most of the Gospels were attributed to it, although we know nothing about Syrian Christianity between 30 and 100 CE except for the little that the much-reviled Luke and Paul report. Between Ignatius (died c.113) and Theophilus of Antioch (c.175 CE) our knowledge is even less. Nevertheless we can find Bultmann saying:

> On this I would merely comment that the problem of the Hellenization of earliest Christianity seems to me to be closely connected with that of its Syrification. The share of Syria in the religious history of Hellenistic and earliest Christian religion is in urgent need of investigation.[10]

Those who as a result of today's widespread preference for Syria put the decisive development of earliest Christianity between 30 and 100 along with the origin of three Gospels (Matthew, Mark and John) there overlook three things:

1. Our knowledge of the Hellenization of Syria in the pre-Christian period is as limited as our knowledge of religious conditions in this province. They do not seem to have changed all that much between the Persian and the Roman period, i.e. between 350 and 50 BCE. Even our knowledge of the capital Antioch, founded as a *polis* in the early Seleucid period, cannot be said to be overwhelming. Apart from the sanctuary of the *Dea Syria* in Hierapolis-Bambyce[11] we have hardly any information about the Syrian cults of that period and virtually no information and no sources at all about pre-Roman 'Hellenistic' Damascus. The situation in the Phoenician cities from Arados to Dor is somewhat better – but only somewhat.[12] We learn by far the most in the period between Alexander and the beginning of the common era about Jews in their mother country and their pagan neighbours. Only on the basis of our knowledge of contemporary Judaism can we report more about the 'environment' or better about the roots of earliest Christianity.

2. 'Syrian' writing proper only begins with Christianity, presumably with Tatian's *Diatessaron*;[13] in other words, with two or three exceptions

around 200 CE we have no non-Christian Syrian literature. Moreover this does not come into being within the territory of the Empire but on its periphery, beyond the Euphrates in Edessa.[14] The great period of Roman Syria begins only in the second century with the cultural activity of the Antonines, and above all in the third century with the rise of the priestly family of Emesa to the imperial throne, the Palmyrene quest for rule and the introduction of the *sol invictus* as imperial god by the Syrian Aurelian. In the first half of the first century CE Syria and its cults were neither particularly creative nor attractive:

> Syria was an intermediary between the high cultures of Egypt, Mesopotamia and Anatolia, but itself for the most part remained a recipient, which produced only sporadic developments of its own.[15]

Only the Phoenician cities became an independently influential cultural and political power.

3. As far as the observers of antiquity were concerned, was not Palestine (or more precisely Judaea and Galilee) part of Syria and very closely bound up with it ethnically, culturally and politically? Up to 200 BCE the Ptolemies could call their territory south of the line between Tripolis and Damascus simply ΣΥΡΙΑ ΚΑΙ ΦΟΙΝΙΚΗ and the Seleucids later could call it ΚΟΙΛΗ ΣΥΡΙΑ. For the Romans Judaea was just a particularly difficult political appendage of the province of Syria. However, for that very reason one must be very cautious about assuming a 'religious' influence from Syrian cults. For Syrian (or Canaanite-Phoenician) paganism, which was to be found immediately alongside them, had long been particularly abhorrent to Jews (and Jewish Christians). Therefore, as is shown by events in Jerusalem and Shechem at the time of Antiochus IV and the *šiqquṣ mᵉšōmem* (Dan.11.31; 9.27 and 12.11, a parody of the Syrian Baal Šamem), even its new form, Hellenized by *interpretatio graeca*, did not change anything.[16] The Baal of Doliche in Commagene and the Syrian sun god had more attention from our forebears in Roman Germania and Britannia than among Jews and Christians in Palestine and Syria. As far as we know,[17] the Syrian cults in Hellenistic garb certainly had no influence on early Christianity in Syria (and Palestine – it is difficult to keep the two apart) geographically.[18] Nor may we simply introduce into the first century the 'orientalizing' of Hellenistic-Roman religious feeling, which becomes visible from the end of the second century and is completely visible in the third. So we can find a truly deep 'Syrian influence' only in the fact that at the end of the third century the late

Roman 'monotheistic' *Sol invictus* became the precursor of Constantine's acceptance of the Christian God.

Against this background, the nomenclature which is quite widespread in contemporary scholarship, based on a fundamental division between 'Palestinian Judaism' and the 'Hellenistic Judaism' of the Diaspora (and especially Syria) and similarly between the earliest 'Palestinian' community and somewhat later the first missionary communities in Syria with a 'Jewish-Christian/Hellenistic' stamp, 'influenced by syncretism', is not completely without problems. The reason for this is as follows.

There is a contrast here between the clear geographical term 'Palestinian' and the relatively indeterminate attribute 'Hellenistic' (though this is to be understood in a cultural and religious sense). At the same time this leaves room for the questionable view that the land of 'Palestine', or an essential part of it, 'Jewish Palestine', was hardly influenced, if at all, by 'Hellenism' – whatever might be understood by that; this in complete contrast to the adjacent areas of Phoenicia, Nabataean Arabia, Syria or Egypt. Underlying the introduction of the keyword 'syncretistic' is the view that this influence included a more or less strong pagan component which may not yet be presupposed in the Palestinian mother country, though it may in the Diaspora of the adjacent regions.

This objection brings us to my specific topic: *What effects of 'Hellenistic' civilization, or more exactly the 'Greek' language, Greek life-style, economy, technology, education, philosophy and religion can be demonstrated in Jewish Palestine in the first century after Christ, i.e. in the time with which we are concerned, during which earliest Christianity came into being,* and predominantly in the *Jewish* parts of Palestine? Here again we need to ask whether it is possible without further ado to make a clear division between 'Jewish' and 'non-Jewish' (or even 'Hellenistic' Palestine) in this way. This topic at the same time contains the question whether 'syncretistic' elements, i.e. the influence of alien culture and religion, were not possible there also (as they had been in earlier Persian and Assyrian times).

Within the limits available here, of course I can only more or less sketch out a selection of perspectives. Essentially, a really thorough investigation of the problem would need a monograph the size of my *Judaism and Hellenism*, the original of which appeared twenty years ago, in which I pursued the problem for the 'early Hellenistic' period as far as the middle or end of the second century. However, instead of the second volume which I promised in the introduction to that book I can only offer a *parergon* which takes up its substantial predecessor.

It is worth noting how often in the sphere of ancient history the countless details have a more or less fortuitous character – though this is not surprising in, for example, discoveries of inscriptions and other archaeological data. But all in all the many 'coincidences', for all their multiplicity, present an amazingly coherent overall picture. Such 'chance discoveries' could be further multiplied by an intensive and systematic search. Moreover I myself am amazed at the degree to which time and again new archaeological and epigraphical discoveries confirm the picture that I once sketched out in *Judaism and Hellenism*.

Here things are most difficult in the sphere of the history of religions, for that is where phenomena are particularly closely interwoven. Here the problem arises in a degree of complexity and complication which is almost impossible to grasp, for at the same time on each occasion one would have to attempt to clarify what the shimmering terms 'Hellenistic', 'Hellenism', 'Hellenization' etc., so beloved of New Testament scholarship, all really mean in their particular historical context. For it is only on that basis that we can say more precisely what were the alleged differences between so-called 'Palestinian' and 'Hellenistic' Judaism, or the earliest 'Palestinian' community and the 'Hellenistic' communities with a Jewish Christian and Gentile Christian stamp. That is to say, if such differences could be clearly demonstrated at all. Can the term 'Hellenistic' be used in a meaningful way for precise distinctions in the history of earliest Christianity generally? Because of this complexity which is so difficult to grasp, to begin with I want to put the history-of-religions question into the background and initially to concentrate primarily on the 'real features' in which the situation can be understood more clearly.

2

The Linguistic Question and its Cultural Background

To begin with the last point: in contrast to the use of 'Hellenizing' and 'Hellenism' stamped by culture and intellectual history which is customary among theologians, and which ultimately goes back to Droysen, in antiquity the verb ἑλληνίζειν and the rare noun Ἑλλη-νισμός referred almost exclusively to language.[19] Only rarely did these words have a comprehensive meaning relating to culture and civilization – with one significant exception to which we shall have to return – and there is evidence of this only in the post-Christian period. In Christian literature from the third-fourth century CE the term Ἕλλην and the other terms associated with it then generally came to mean 'pagan'.[20] Before that both terms primarily and in the first instance denoted an impeccable command of the Greek language. This also gives us a first fairly clear criterion for distinction in this investigation: *'Hellenistic' Jews and Jewish Christians are (in the real, original meaning of the word) those whose mother tongue was Greek*,[21] in contrast to the Jews in Palestine and in the Babylonian Diaspora who originally spoke Aramaic. It is in this way, in terms of mother tongue, that Luke understands the distinction between Ἑλληνισταί and Ἑβραῖοι in Acts 6.1 (cf. 9.29).[22] The mother- (or main) language of the Ἡλληνισταί is Greek and that of the Ἑβραῖοι Aramaic. However, we meet these two groups in Jerusalem itself, in the Jewish metropolis of the Holy Land – and that goes against the usual dividing line. It is too easily forgotten that in the time of Jesus Greek had already been established as a language for more than three hundred years and already had a long and varied history behind it. As early as the third century in different parts of Palestine we have a whole series of testimonies to Greek as a language, and they are slowly but steadily continuing to increase in number.[23] The Greek language had already long been accepted not only in the former Philistine or Phoenician areas on the coast and (in the third century BCE) in the 'Graeco-Macedonian' cities in the interior, but also (though not so intensively) in areas settled by Jews and Samaritans. Judaea, Samaria and Galilee were bilingual (or better, trilingual) areas. While Aramaic was the vernacular of ordinary people,[24] and Hebrew the sacred language of religious worship and of scribal discussion, Greek had largely become established as the lingustic medium for trade, commerce and administration.

The victorious Maccabaean revolt and the national and religious renewal associated with it had hardly changed anything in this respect. Here is an elementary example of this. The Hasmonaean high priest and king Alexander Jannaeus (103-76 BCE), who enjoyed political success generally, already issued what were presumably the first Jewish bilingual coins, with *y⁽ʰônatan hak-kohen hag-gadol* on one side and ΒΑΣΙΛΕΩΣ ᾿ΑΛΕΞΑΝΔΡΟΥ on the other.[25] His grandson, the last Hasmonaean king Mattathias Antigonus, during the time of his desperate war against Herod and the Romans in 40-37 BCE, followed the same practice. The contemporary Nabataean king Aretas III similarly minted bilingual coins with the legend ΒΑΣΙΛΕΩΣ ΑΡΕΤΟΥ ΦΙΛΕΛΛΗΝΟΣ,[26] but his successors again limited themselves to Nabataean until the annexation of their kingdom by Trajan in 106 CE. That King Aretas IV, Paul's contemporary (II Cor.11.32), minted coins with the Nabataean legend 'lover of his (own) people' (*rḥm ῾mh*) seems to be an expression of national feeling and amounts to an implicit rejection of such titles as φιλορώμαιος and φιλέλληνος. We do not find such nationalistic confessions on the coins of the Jewish kings.

Herod then went over to purely Greek inscriptions on Jewish coins and weights, as did his sons and the Roman procurators. It was only the rebels in 66-70 and 132-195 who returned to coins with legends in ancient Hebrew. By contrast, Greek inscriptions had been a matter of course for Ptolemaic and Seleucid money and for the coins minted by 'Hellenistic' cities in Palestine itself since the third century BCE; the only exception here were the Phoenician cities, which were very conscious of their status and tradition.[27]

S.Krauss's work on loanwords from Greek and Latin in rabbinic literature, i.e. from the second century CE, contains 'around 3000 items... and these extend over the whole realm of human language'.[28] In his temperamental polemic against Bousset's *Religion des Judentums* F.Perles speaks of 1100 Greek loanwords in rabbinic literature, which 'also in other respects at many points betrays a deeper knowledge of Greek and Roman cultural life'.[29] However, the earliest Greek loanwords do not appear only in the Mishnah; if we leave aside the musical instruments in Daniel (3.5,10,15, see n.15) and the drachmae (*dark'mōnīm*) in Ezra 2.69 and Nehemiah 7.69-71 they already occur in the copper scroll of Qumran.[30] Greek money had already come into the country at the beginning of the Persian period (or even earlier).[31]

The linguistic problem was discussed at length by Sevenster[32] in a monograph in 1968 and has long been familiar to scholars, though one continually gets the impression that its consequences for the New Testament have often not been fully taken into account. The constant discovery of new inscriptions confirms this picture of a fundamentally multilingual society. Schlatter already drew attention to this situation in his famous study on 'The Language and Homeland of the Fourth Evangelist' (which is in no way taken seriously enough):

> Here too the inscriptions are the decisive authority for assessing the linguistic question (of a bilingual situation, M.H.). The fact that we do not have any from west of the Jordan is made up for by the inscriptions from the Hauran.[33]

In the meantime we also have two bilingual inscriptions from Judaea and Galilee, quite apart from the large number of testimonies to use of the Greek language. Almost ninety years ago Schlatter had a completely correct view of the linguistic situation, a clearer one than the representatives of the History of Religions school.

The most important centre of the Greek language in Jewish Palestine was of course the capital, Jerusalem. We again have a good deal of epigraphical evidence to support this.

Thus we have a number of public inscriptions in Greek from the period of the Second Temple, above all the two famous warning inscriptions which prohibit Gentiles from entering the inner precincts of the Temple (*CIJ* 2,1400), and in addition we now also have an honorific inscription, which is presumably dedicated to a donor from the Jewish community in Rhodes who paid for a stone pavement (in the Temple?).[34] The *earliest* Greek inscription in Jerusalem comes from an even earlier period, presumably from the Seleucid military settlers in the Acra in Jerusalem.[35] In addition there are a large number of Greek epitaphs from Jerusalem: a good third were written in Greek.[36] My colleague L.Y.Rahmani of Jerusalem was kind enough to write me a letter giving the latest information from the catalogue of Jewish ossuaries from Jerusalem and its environs which is in process of publication (letter of 1 November 1988):

> Of the 872 inscriptions in the catalogue, 228 have writing on them: 138 of these are in Jewish script, 71 in Greek, 15 (or 16) in both, 2 in Latin, 1 in Palmyrene. It should be observed that from many groups of graves often only the ossuaries with writing or ornaments on them found their way into the collection; the majority bear neither decoration nor inscription.

Formal phrases in Aramaic rarely appear, as Rahmani explains in the introduction to one item in the catalogue:

> 'It may, however, still be significant that of the few formulas appearing containing a short warning intended to protect the remains of the deceased, one – short and simple – is in Aramaic, while three are contained in a somewhat larger Greek sentence... consolatory inscriptions are represented by a sole Aramaic epigram, clearly influenced by Greek in contents and literary form (!).[37] In a few bilinguals, the main inscription is the one in Greek, the Hebrew one added being short, as though merely summarizing the main information...' In a Greek warning inscription with a quotation from Deut.28.28 or Zech.12.4 the writer evidently could not recall the Greek expression (ἀορασία/ἀποτύφλωσις) 'and thus transcribed the Hebrew *'wrwn* as οὐρον. In general one can thus summarize that the meagre evidence emerging from the ossuary inscriptions as to the knowledge of Greek in Jerusalem and Jericho and their environments is at the time in question rather similar to that noted for a somewhat later period at Beth She'arim: little systematic knowledge of language, grammar or literature, but rather a knowledge of speech, probably also in everyday use; and this also by lower classes of the local Jewish population.'

If one counts the bilingual texts as Greek, the number of Greek (and Latin) ossuary inscriptions in Jerusalem and its environs amounts to 39%. If one proceeds on the basis that it would make sense for only those ossuaries to be inscribed in Greek in the case of which the dead or their families used Greek as the vernacular or their mother tongue, we may put the proportion of the population as a whole at around 10-20% as a minimum. In a population of between 80,000 and 100,000 inhabitants that would give a number of between 8,000 and 16,000 Greek-speaking Jews in greater Jerusalem,[38] to which would be added the numerous pilgrims from the Diaspora who lodged in the city at the great festivals. Given so great a proportion of Greek speakers in the population, we have to assume an independent Jewish Hellenistic culture in Jerusalem and its environs, which was different from that of Alexandria or Antioch. We shall be coming back to this significant point on a number of occasions.

The few place names which appear on the ossuary inscriptions in no way indicate that the dead came exclusively from the Diaspora; alongside places like Alexandria, Cyrene (possibly including the family of Simon of Cyrene)[39] and Capua in Italy, good Palestinian places like Bethel and Scythopolis/Beth-shean also appear.[40] The tomb of the 'Goliath family' in Jericho is a sensation; it contains more Greek inscriptions and names than Aramaic and the most important person it mentions is a 'Theodotus, freeman of the empress Agrippina', i.e. the wife of the Emperor Claudius and mother of Nero; by contrast his wife and daughter have simple Aramaic names.[41] The Greek names are better written than the Aramaic ones. In addition there is also mention of a number of proselytes in Jerusalem.[42] The situation is different with the later synagogue inscriptions scattered round the country, extending from the first century to the seventh. Here Greek inscriptions (around 30) are to be found predominantly in the cities, while there are about 110 Hebrew (and Aramaic) inscriptions in the numerous synagogues all over the country, above all in Galilee and the Golan. Of course people were relatively conservative in worship.[43] Here, too, again it is not sheer chance that the earliest synagogue inscription that we know from Jewish Palestine (at the same time it is the only one so far to come from Jerusalem), the Theodotus inscription, is written in Greek. The ruler of the synagogue and priest Theodotus, son of Vettenus, is presumably descended from Jewish freemen from Rome (*gens Vettena*).[44] We shall be frequently be concerned with this important text later.

This special significance of the Greek language in Jerusalem in the first centuries before and after Christ is no coincidence. In the time of Herod and the Roman prefects or procurators up to the Jewish war Jerusalem was not only the capital of Jewish Palestine but was at the same time a metropolis of international, world-wide significance, a great 'attraction' in the literal sense, the centre of the whole inhabited world. Nor was it the 'navel' only for pious Jews of the Diaspora but also an interesting place for educated Greeks, pagans and adventurers.[45]

The court of Herod, which was entirely dominated by the spirit of Hellenism and game-hunting, gymnastics, musical performances, dramatic spectacles, chariot races... all constituted a powerful centre of attraction for strangers. Foreigners who took an active or a passive part in the contests, writers and other educated Greeks, were guests at the Herodian court. To these were added the many official connections which Herod maintained, as did Agrippa I; these brought ambassadors, messengers and foreign bodyguards.[46]

With splendid buildings in the style of Hellenistic architecture the city could stand comparison with the prestigious buildings of other major Hellenistic cities, indeed it even surpassed these. The discoveries in excavations in the Jewish Old City of Jerusalem and on the former Temple Mount have produced an eloquent example of this.[47] Alongside the use of Greek was the 'language of forms' represented by the predominant Hellenistic architecture and domestic culture. The excavations of a building like a palace on the east side of the West Hill, with ornamental wall-paintings in the second style of Pompeii,[48] illustrate the quality of domestic life among the upper classes in Jerusalem. The discovery of a beautiful Corinthian and Ionian capital[49] in the excavations in the old city demonstrate the extent and the quality of Hellenistic provincial architecture. The same is true of the tombs in the Kidron valley which have already been known for a long time.[50] In the case of the capitals the degree of perfection of the style, compared with the still relatively simple Hasmonaean tombs, is striking.

Money flowed into the city from the didrachma tax, which Herod had had safely transferred to Jerusalem thanks to the *pax Romana*,[51] and a good deal more money came into the city through the sacrifices of the festival pilgrims. The temple with its bank was one of the richest in antiquity, and time and again tempted Roman generals and officials to lay hands on its treasure. The Jewish population reacted to this sacrilege with disturbances.[52] The daily life of at least the upper classes fully matched the standard of luxury and comfort to which people in the Roman empire were accustomed.[53]

Pausanias says that the tomb of Queen Helena of Adiabene in Parthia, who with her son Izates and other members of her family had gone over to Judaism, could be compared only with the tomb of King Mausolus in Halicarnassus, which was one of the seven wonders of the world.[54] Her son, King Izates, sent five sons to be educated in the Holy City (Josephus, *Antt.* 20.71). Two relatives of Izates' brother and successor Monobazus, who like his mother and brother had also gone over to Judaism (20.75), fell on the Jewish side during the defence of the city in 70 CE (*BJ* 2.520), and other sons and brothers of Izates surrendered shortly before the conquest of the capital by the Romans and were brought to Rome as hostages (*BJ* 6.356).

So Jerusalem was without doubt one of the most impressive and famous temple cities in the Roman empire, and even for pagans was surrounded with an almost 'mystical' aura.[55]

The number of pilgrims from the Diaspora at the great festivals exceeded that of the inhabitants.[56] Even Philo who visited Jerusalem at least once (fragment of *De Providentia*, in Eusebius, *PE VIII*, 14.64), calls it his real 'ancestral city (πατρίς), the metropolis not only of a Jewish land but of most other lands because of the colonies which it... sent out' (*Leg.Gai.* 281, cf. *Flacc.* 46; *Leg.Gai.* 203, etc.).

It was probably the particular achievement of Herod, who had taken over the role of patron of Diaspora Judaism, that he helped the Holy City to have this international significance in the Roman empire, a significance which impressed even pagans and which he strengthened by his restless building activity in the Graeco-Roman style.[57]

Presumably he also facilitated the return of prominent Diaspora Jews. Thus the beginnings of the synagogue of Theodotus, which is perhaps connected with that of the 'Libertines', i.e. the Roman freemen of Acts 6.9, and which is known to us through the famous inscription of the grandson of the founder, who completed it, go back to Herodian times.[58] The building included not only the liturgical room 'for reading out the law and instruction in the commandments', but a hospice and arrangements for ritual bathing for pilgrims 'from abroad'. There were certainly also other 'diaspora synagogues' in the city.[59] Acts 6.9 mentions some of them, in first place that of the Λιβερτῖνοι, i.e. the Jewish freemen from Rome. Perhaps the synagogue of Theodotus and that of the Libertines are identical.

In these Greek-speaking synagogue communities in Jerusalem the Septuagint was used, and while on the one hand there was teaching in the style of the Hellenistic Judaism of Alexandria, on the other there was an attempt to make the understanding of the Law which was predominant among the Pharisees in Palestine known to the festival pilgrims from the Diaspora. This is the environment in which Sha'ul-Paul from Tarsus will have grown up (Acts 22.4; cf.26.4; Rom.15.19).[60] To some degree the variety of Judaism as a whole, including the Diaspora, was therefore best represented in Jerusalem. People met there from all parts of the Roman empire: Rome, Asia Minor, Antioch and Egypt (Acts 2.9-11; cf.6.9), but also from Babylonia, Media and *Arabia felix*. The finance minister of the Ethiopian kingdom of Napata-Meroe (Acts 8.27),[61] presumably a godfearer, was one example among many.

There was a constant and lively interchange with all the centres of the Diaspora. Thus Herod first brought the priest Ananel (Josephus, *Antiquities* 15.22, 34, 39ff., 51) from Babylonia and later the priest Simon, son of Boethus, from Alexandria to Jerusalem, both presumably from the old Zadokite family of the Oniads, in order to appoint them high priests.[62] Boethus could have been a descendant of Onias IV of Leontopolis who fled to Egypt in 164 BCE: that would explain the later status of his family in Jerusalem. The successful Simon, son of Boethus, who married a daughter, Mariamne, to Herod, succeeded in founding the richest high priestly family after the clan of Annas and at the same time a particular group among the Sadducees, the Boethusians, who were evidently close to the Herodian rulers. The bones of the rich Alexandrian Nicanor, who had the doors of the Nicanor gate made,[63] were also laid to rest in Jerusalem. Possibly, like the proselytes from the royal house of Adiabene (see above, p.12f.), he had come to live there in his old age. A more recent interpretation conjectures that the remains of his sons Nicanor and Alexas found rest in the inscribed ossuary.[64]

Be this as it may, we can assume that Greek was spoken among the families of these aristocrats who had returned. It will also be the case that Greek was no less established among the leading families of Jerusalem than in the scriptoria and the bazaars of the city or at the tables of the money changers in the temple forecourt.[65]

However, the significance of language was not just limited to Jerusalem. Thus a substantial Jewish population lived in the Hellenized cities of the coastal plain from Gaza to Dor or Ptolemais-Acco: in Caesarea they made up almost half the population, and in Jamnia certainly and Ashdod probably they outnumbered the Hellenized Gentile population.[66] Philip, who came from the group around Stephen, may have preached primarily in Greek in the coastal plain and particularly in Caesarea.[67] That Greek was the principal language in these cities is again confirmed by Jewish epitaphs and synagogue inscriptions.[68]

The same may also be true of Pella, Samaria-Sebaste and the only *poleis* founded by Antipas in Galilee: Tiberias and Sepphoris.[69] Galilee,[70] completely encircled by the territories of the Hellenized cities of Ptolemais, Tyre and Sidon in the west and north-west, by Panias-Caesarea Philippi, Hippos and Gadara in the north-east, east and south-east,[71] and finally by Scythopolis and Gaba, a military settlement founded by Herod,[72] in the south, will similarly have been largely bilingual. Scythopolis, the old Beth-shean, presumably derived its remarkable name from the fact that in the third century BCE the Ptolemies settled cavalry there from the kingdom on the Bosphorus ('Scythians').[73] Under the mythical name Nysa it was a particular cult place of Dionysus; according to tradition the nurse of the god was buried there.[74] On coins and in an inscription the city calls itself Ἑλληνὶς πόλις, which is perhaps meant to guard against a misunderstanding of the place name: in antiquity the Scythians were regarded as the barbarians *par excellence*.[75] Pompey restored the city, which had been sacked by Alexander Jannaeus; it was the only city west of the Jordan to be incorporated into the Decapolis. Anyone who wants to discover Dionysian features in John 2.1-11 should not forget that there was an old centre of Dionysus worship about eighteen miles southeast of Cana and Nazareth,[76] and a mosaic with a Dionysus cycle on it has also recently been excavated in Sepphoris (though this is later: third century CE).[77] In Hellenistic, pre-Roman times Tell Anafa-Arsinoe flourished just next to the northern frontier in the eastern part of the Hule valley.[78] It was presumably destroyed by Alexander Jannaeus around 80 BCE. Another Hellenistic city founded by the Ptolemies which disappeared when it was conquered by the Hasmonaeans was Philotheria (Beth-Jerach) at the south end of Lake Tiberias. When Antiochus III captured it in 220 BCE it was a significant fortress (Polybius, 5.70.3f.). Because of its Greek name, Tarichaea, the Jewish Magdala, around four miles north of Tiberias on the same lake, seems to have been a Hellenistic foundation as the centre of the fishing industry. As early as Herodotus, ταριχεῖαι are probably factories for the production of salt fish.[79] Presumably there was a whole series of smaller Macedonian-Greek settlements in Palestine which did not develop into real cities and did not have any rights as cities.[80] In economic terms Galileee was to a large extent dependent on the completely Hellenized Phoenician cities, especially Acco/Ptolemais and Tyre. The great cemetery in Beth-shearim between Nazareth and Haifa which comes from between the second and fourth centuries CE contains predominantly Greek inscriptions.[81] Some of those buried there come from the Phoenician metropolises. After the death of R.Jehuda han-Nasi (after 200) the tombs of Beth-shearim took on a more than regional significance, like the Holy City before 70 CE. The marked increase in Greek inscriptions compared to those in Hebrew and Aramaic (218 to 28) is bound up with the further development of the process of Hellenization in the second to fourth centuries CE, the proximity to Phoenician cities and the social structure of the users, who evidently quite overwhelmingly came from the upper class. We may assume that the rabbinic teachers from the Tannaitic period all *also* spoke Greek.

The letters of Bar Kosiba from the wilderness of Judaea have provided us with further material; they show that the Jewish pseudo-messiah (or one of his officers) got on better in Greek than in Hebrew.[82]

We may also draw conclusions from this background for the Jesus movement. Among the twelve disciples of Jesus two, Andrew and Philip, bear purely Greek names, and in the case of two others the original Greek name has been Aramaized. Thaddaeus (*tadda'j*) is probably a short form of Theodotus (or something similar), and Bartholomew (*Bartholomaios = bar-talmaj*) derives from (bar) Ptolemaios. The blind beggar Bartimaeus (Bar-Timaios) in Jericho, who becomes a follower of Jesus, can also be mentioned in this connection.[83] Such Greek names are often attested for Jews in Palestine and Egypt. Shimᵉ'on/Simon, the most frequent Jewish name in Palestine, was so prized because on the one hand it recalled the most successful Maccabaean brother who achieved independence and founded the Hasmonaean dynasty, and on the other hand it could be turned into Greek without any trouble. Shimᵉ'on and Simon were almost interchangeable.[84] The information that Simon Peter, Andrew and Philip came from Bethsaida (John 1.44) could perhaps have historical value, since Herod's son Philip refounded this place soon after his accession as the *polis Julias* (before 2 BCE) in honour of Augustus' daughter Julia and it was therefore more markedly 'Hellenized' than the surrounding villages.[85] The name Philip was then presumably a token of respect to the ruler of the country, who according to Josephus, *Antiquities* 18.106f., was regarded as being particularly just.[86] The place seems to have had some significance in the first century, even if it could not maintain this in the long run. At all events, Simon Peter must have been bilingual, since otherwise he could not have engaged so successfully in missionary work outside Judaea from Antioch via Corinth to Rome. It is remarkable that Luke does not know of Peter having any problems with language – say in connection with Cornelius; this arises for him only in the case of Paul before the crowd in Jerusalem and the tribune Claudius Lysias (Acts 21.37,40; cf. also 22.2).[87]

Of course there was a knowledge of Greek especially among the upper classes, though the quality of this knowledge varied quite considerably, from the basic knowledge need to make oneself understood to higher literary skills which few possessed – we shall go into this in more detail later. Such knowledge was a prerequisite for upward social mobility, both in crafts and trade and in the service of the political powers, the Herodian rulers, the cities, the temple administration and the other Jewish authorities and even more in the service of Rome. The better the knowledge of language a Palestinian Jew acquired, the more easily he could rise in the social scale.

The larger cities, primarily Jerusalem, but also Sepphoris and Tiberias, had Greek schools which presumably went as far as an elementary training in rhetoric. An institution like the temple must have had a well-staffed Greek secretariat for more than two centuries (see below, 22f.).

From the beginning, those trained in such schools with a higher social status gained particular significance for the Jesus movement. We may assume that Jesus himself, who as a building craftsman belonged to the middle class, and to an even greater degree his brother James, was capable of carrying on a conversation in Greek. The synoptic tradition presupposes without further ado that he could talk with the captain from Capernaum, Pilate or the Syro-Phoenician woman ('Ελληνίς, Mark 7.26).[88] The situation of his native Nazareth on the border of Galilee and five kilometres from Sepphoris, the old capital of the region, offered a variety of possibilities of contacts with non-Jews. Possibly as a building craftsman (ὁ τέκτων, Mark 6.3)[89] Jesus worked on the rebuilding of Sepphoris.[90]

However, we do not necessarily have to go so far as Zahn, G.Kittel and J.N.Sevenster[91] in supposing that James in any case himself wrote his letter, composed in excellent Greek, even if the the good style is not in itself an argument against a Palestinian origin for the letter. As leader of the earliest community in Jerusalem he could certainly also have had the use of a secretary. The discussion at the 'apostolic council' will at least have been carried on *also* in Greek, otherwise the presence of a Greek like Titus will hardly have made sense. We can therefore spare ourselves the hypothesis of an Aramaic protocol[92] from which Paul is supposed to be quoting.

There are many references to what were in all probability bilingual members of the community from the upper and middle classes: mention should be made of Johanna, the wife of Chuza, the 'ἐπίτροπος of Herod Antipas, i.e. his steward; the tax farmers, like the ἀρχιτελώνης Zacchaeus in Jericho; then men like Nicodemus and Joseph of Arimathaea. The mysterious Manaen (Menachem) in Antioch, whose mother is perhaps mentioned by Papias,[93] the boyhood friend (? σύντροφος) of Herod Antipas, Mary and her son John Mark, the relations of Barnabas, Silas-Silvanus, Barsabbas Justus, who similarly emerges again in Papias,[94] the prophet Agabus and others may similarly belong in this milieu. Their circle is enlarged by Diaspora Jews resident in Jerusalem like Barnabas from Cyprus, and Simon of Cyrene with his sons Alexander and Rufus. Simon's sons and his mother were perhaps known later in the Christian community in Rome,[95] and Jason of Cyprus, Paul's host (Acts 21.16), whose mother tongue was already Greek, even if they still understood Aramaic or had relearned it. Not least, mention should of course be made here of the 'Seven' as the spokesmen of the Hellenist community (Acts 6.5), who all have Greek names, and naturally – above all others as far as his effect on the Christian church and world history is concerned – of Sha'ul/ Paul, who studied the Torah in Jerusalem and persecuted the community of Christian 'Hellenists'.[96]

These levels of bilinguality would also explain why, presumably even during the lifetime of Jesus, the message of Jesus also reached Diaspora Jews in Jerusalem who almost only spoke Greek or spoke it exclusively; it was from among them that that group of Hellenists was recruited which separated because of its worship in Greek and as a special group in the community became significant in Jerusalem with such amazing rapidity. John 12.20f. could be a later reflection of this transition. Perhaps John 4.38 is a reference to their mission in Samaria (Acts 8.4ff.). At all events it is probable that the rendering of parts of the Jesus tradition into Greek and the development of a distinctive theological terminology with terms like ἀπόστολος, εὐαγγέλιον, ἐκκλησία, χάρις, χάρισμα, ὁ υἱὸς τοῦ ἀνθρώπου, etc. must have begun very early, possibly as an immediate consequence of the activity of Jesus, which also attracted Diaspora Jews, in Jerusalem, and not, say, decades later outside Palestine in Antioch or elsewhere. In other words, the roots of the 'Jewish-Christian/Hellenistic' or more precisely the Greek-speaking Jewish Christian community in which the message of Jesus was formulated in Greek for the first time clearly extend back to the very earliest community in Jerusalem, and accordingly the first linguistic development of its kerygma and its christology must have already taken place there.

3
Greek Education and Literature in Jewish Palestine

Henri Irénée Marrou defined the Hellenistic world between Alexander and the early empire as a 'civilization of *paideia*'.[97] At this point we encounter a converging tendency which dominated both the Jewish wisdom schools with their invitation to accept *mūsār* and learn *ḥokhmā*, and the new Graeco-Macedonian plantation cities of the new world with their ideal of education.[98] Though the goal of education might initially be different, indeed contrary, in the long run there could not fail to be an influence of each side on the other. As social status and professional success for orientals – Syrians, Phoenicians, Egyptians or Jews – to a great extent depended on an acceptance of the elements of Greek education, to begin with Greek influence was greater. Indeed if we leave Judaism aside as a special case, the Greek element in education was dominant in the upper classes of Syria and Palestine – which were the only important ones. Here Fergus Millar stresses a point which we must keep in mind if we are to have a correct estimation of the spiritual power of the Judaism of that time:

> One of the most successful achievements of Graeco-Roman civilization was the removal of the memories and identities of the people whom it absorbed. Alone of all the peoples under Roman rule, the Jews not only had a long recorded history but kept it, re-interpreted it and acted on it.[99]

But even where there was opposition and conflict involving vigorous argument with the new pagan civilization, as in Judaism, people became more strongly 'infected' by it than they realized.[100]

If we want to define the difficult concept of 'Hellenization' more closely, over and above the dissemination of the Greek language but in the closest connection with it, we come up against the ideal of Greek education, regardless of whether we want to understand it more in terms of technology, military matters and sports and the gymnasium, or in terms of rhetorical, literary and philosophical education. The religious motive which interests theologians most here fades into the background – at least to begin with.

It is amazing how many significant Greek academics, men of letters and thinkers were produced by the new Graeco-Macedonian foundations or the Graecized cities of Palestine and Transjordan from the second century BCE onwards. Gadara, about six miles from the southern border of Galilee as the crow flies, was the home town of Menippus, the inventor of satire from the fourth to third century BCE;[101] Meleager, the founder of the Greek anthology from the second century;[102] and the Epicurean Philodemus, for whose library we are indebted to the papyrus discoveries in Herculaneum, from the first century BCE.[103] The orator Theodore of Gadara, who instructed the future emperor Tiberius, lived at the end of the first century BCE,[104] and at the beginning of the second century CE the Cynic Oenomaus of Gadara,[105] who is presumably mentioned in a very positive way in the Talmud, but also meets with the approval of Eusebius, so that he hands down some substantial passages about him in his *Praeparatio Evangelica*.[106] In an epigram Meleager praises the city as the 'Athens of Syria',[107] and an epitaph from Hippo calls it χρηστομουσία, 'an excellent abode of learning'.[108] Stephen of Byzantium lists two orators and a sophist as coming from Gerasa, and the neo-Pythagorean and mathematician Nicomachus from the second century CE is particularly well known.[109] As coming from Ashkelon, the only coastal city, which the Hasmonaeans were unable to capture,[110] Stephen of Byzantium mentions not only the well known Antiochus, who revived Platonism and was a contemporary of Cicero,[111] but also three Stoic philosophers, two grammarians and two historians. The grammarian Ptolemaeus taught in Rome during the early period of the Empire. Even if these scholars did not usually remain in the country but made their fortunes in the cultural centres of the West, we must assume that there was a firm and lasting scholarly tradition in the places I have mentioned – to which should also be added the Phoenician cities of Tyre and Sidon, which while preserving their own tradition at the same time achieved a considerable cultural climax. All these towns provided a solid education and also enjoyed an influence to match.

Even Jewish Palestine could not escape the attraction of Greek education, which flourished in the Hellenistic cities all around it. Here we must also take into account the growing influence of the most significant centres of the Greek-speaking Diaspora like Alexandria, Antioch and Rome, but also the nearby Phoenician cities. The starting point was a basic elementary instruction in grammar by the γραμματιστής, which could also be given in Judaea. The author of the *Letter of Aristeas*, writing in Alexandria, takes it for granted around 140 BCE that the seventy-two translators who came from Palestine had all had a solid Greek education, and conversely the Talmudic literature also knows the Septuagint legends in their more developed form, corresponding to that in Philo, in which each individual translator was inspired.[112] The contrary verdict to this very positive interpretation, that the composition of the Septuagint had been a catastrophe for Israel, like the day on which the golden calf was made, only shows that at a later date the question of the significance of the Greek Bible was controversial in Palestinian Judaism itself and that it was not used there without objections. After the second century CE it was increasingly rejected because of the rivalry of the Christians and replaced by Aquila's translation. There can be no doubt that it was used frequently in Jerusalem, probably in the synagogue of Theodotus. Fragments of Greek translations of the Hebrew Bible have been found both in Qumran and in the Wadi Murabba'at,[113] and in addition numerous Greek legal texts have been found in the Wadi Murabba'at and Nahal Hever.[114] The scroll of the twelve prophets from Wadi Murabba'at[115] indicates that at an earlier stage, long before Aquila, Theodotion and Symmachus, the revisions in the second century CE, there were distinctive Palestinian recensions of the Septuagint which corrected the text with philological accuracy on the basis of the Hebrew original. The editors must have learned their Greek grammar well. Paul himself was already working with such a revised text of the books of Isaiah, Job and Kings, and it is quite possible that he made this critical revision himself.[116] One can no longer make use of the Septuagint as an indication that a text came into being outside Palestine; indeed it is necessary to ask whether later parts of it were not translated in Palestine (see below, 24f.).

However, the influence of Greek education and literature extends very much wider. We already find it in late Hebrew and Aramaic literature, for example in Koheleth, Ben Sira, Daniel or the Enoch writings. The first Palestinian Jewish author known to us who wrote in Greek, the anonymous Samaritan,[117] was writing at the time of Ben Sira. He identifies Enoch, the primal sage of Gen.5.22, with Atlas, the brother of Prometheus, who was similarly regarded as an outstanding astronomer, mathematician and philosopher. King Nimrod of Babylon is associated in euhemeristic fashion with the God Bel in Babylon, and Abraham becomes the one who brought the cult to Phoenicia and Egypt, and therefore indirectly to the Greeks also. It was in this early period, presumably in Jerusalem and on the basis of a Jewish initiative, that the legend came into being of the primal affinity between Jews and Spartans through Abraham.[118] The Graecizing of Jerusalem as Ἱεροσόλυμα is along the same lines; the designation first identified the city as a Hellenistic holy temple city, 'the holy Solyma' (ἱερόπολις, Philo, *Leg.Gai.* 225, 281, etc.), and secondly associated it with the 'canonical' primal document of the Greeks, the *Iliad*, in which the 'glorious Solymi' appear (6.184), while according to *Odyssey* 5.283 the Solymi mountains are near to Ethiopia. Such interpretations were to exalt the significance of the city and the Jewish people in the eyes of the Greeks.[119]

The building of a gymnasium at the foot of the temple mount and the attempt to transform Jerusalem into a Greek polis with the right of Antiochene citizenship, both of which were prompted by the high priest Jason in 175 BCE, show how far the 'Hellenization' of the upper class through Greek *paideia* had already developed by that time.[120] In this connection Jason of Cyrene speaks in II Macc.4.13 of an ἀκμή τις Ἑλληνισμοῦ, 'a climax of attempts at Hellenization', in so doing using the term Ἑλληνισμός for the first time in a cultural sense as synonymous with ἀλλοφυλισμός. It is significant that this change of meaning was brought about by a Jew, just as the composite verb ἀφελληνίζειν in the wider cultural sense of 'Hellenize' appears for the first time in Philo (*Leg.Gai.* 147). In other words the Jews were particularly sensitive to the all-pervading and infectious power of the new civilization.

We must expect that already at that time, at the beginning of the second century BCE, there will have been a very effective Greek elementary school in Jerusalem, since Greek 'basic education' was the necessary precondition for a gymnasium and the training of ephebes in accordance with 'Greek custom'.

Both the Greek elementary school and the Greek scriptorium had already found an established place in the Jewish capital from the third century BCE, even during and after the Maccabaean revolt (see above, 17). This was already called for by the international status and reputation of the temple city and the political and religious propaganda of the Hasmonaeans, Herod and the temple hierarchy in the Graeco-Roman world. For this reason the Hasmonaeans also continued to be interested in the preservation of Spartan legend (see below, 77 n.118). The presumably forged letter of the people of Jerusalem under the leadership of Judas Maccabaeus to Aristobulus and the Jews in Alexandria in II Macc.2.14f. refers to the temple library newly set up by Judas Maccabaeus and invites the Alexandrians to make use of it when they need, presumably using writings in Greek.[121] Around the middle of the second century BCE the Jewish Palestinian priest Eupolemus, son of John, whom Judas had probably sent to Rome with a delegation in 161 BCE, composed in Greek a Jewish history with the title 'About the Kings of Judah' despite, indeed perhaps because of, the Maccabaean fight for freedom, to the greater glory of freedom-loving Jews.

B.Z.Wacholder, who analyses this work,[122] goes very thoroughly in the last chapter of his book[123] into further Jewish-Palestinian literature in Greek and traces it down to Justus of Tiberias and Josephus. In his view, its origin lies in the priestly aristocracy, the leading representatives of which had always also had a certain degree of Greek education from the second or even third century BCE. It had its focus in a markedly nationalistic historiography orientated on the sanctuary, and its greatest representative, Josephus, was also its last – because of the destruction of the temple and the annihilation of the priestly nobility. Diaspora Judaism did not produce anything comparable in the Greek language in the sphere of Jewish historiography. Its most important historian, Jason of Cyrene, author of a five-volume history of the origins and beginnings of the Maccabaean revolt, which an unknown writer summarized in II Maccabees, was similarly completely orientated on the history of Palestinian Judaism and was presumably living in Judaea during the revolt (see below, 25f.).[124]

By contrast, as a Jerusalem priest, Josephus, who was proud of his Hasmonaean descent,[125] must already have received the basic foundation of his amazingly broad Greek education in the holy city; it enabled him as a young man to undertake a mission to the imperial court which introduced him to the Empress Poppaea and which ultimately became very successful.[126] No one would ever have been chosen for such a purpose whose Greek was tortuous. However, he had to resort even later to literary helpers in his literary works (but not in the *Vita* and *Contra Apionem*). Still, as a rule non-German doctoral candidates from the Anglo-Saxon world have to do that, even if they have already lived in Germany for years. And for a Semite Greek was even more difficult to learn. Despite their outwardly Hellenistic garb, Josephus's later works – above all the *Antiquities* and *Contra Apionem* – are very much more markedly stamped by Palestinian haggadah and halakah than for example the exegetical works of Philo. Therefore Josephus stresses at the end of his *Antiquities* that his Jewish education was more perfect than his Greek, and that he still found difficulties in speaking impeccable Greek (*Antt.* 20.262-4) – here an English-speaking Swabian can have sympathies. Presumably he also refers to this deficiency because his rival and opponent Justus of Tiberias had had a better linguistic and rhetorical education. Josephus had to stress this against his will (*Vita* 40). The patriarch Photius of Constantinople (c.820-886) still praised the stylistic precision and evocative character of Justus' history of the Jewish kings, which extended from Moses to the death of Agrippa II, the last Jewish king.[127]

Wachholder believes that the rhetorical training which Justus received in the Tiberias of Herod Antipas and Agrippa II was on a par with the 'cosmopolitan Greek of Antioch or Alexandria',[128] whereas Jerusalem could not offer Josephus educational possibilities of the same high quality. I would doubt that, since we do not know whether the young priest Joseph ben Mattathiahu initially had a particular interest in an advanced rhetorical training, or whether with the arrogance of a member of the priestly aristocracy he did not begin by contenting himself with learning to speak and write *koine* Greek fluently.[129] According to his *Vita*, as a young man he concentrated more on the study of the Jewish tradition, including the Essenes.[130]

There is no question that there is a substantial difference between the style of Eupolemus, which is still 'Jewish-Greek' and close to that of the Septuagint, and that of the last two Jewish historians. The level of the Jewish scribal school in Jerusalem in Maccabaean-Hasmonaean times was probably not yet (or no longer) on a par with grammatical and rhetorical training; it was a more workmanlike affair, as too are the translations of the various books of the Greek Bible. The colophon to the Greek book of Esther shows that the rendering of the books of the Old Testament, the Apocrypha and Pseudepigrapha into Greek need not always have taken place in the Greek-speaking Diaspora, above all in Alexandria.

> In the fourth year of the reign of Ptolemaeus and Cleopatra, Dositheus who, as he said, was a priest and levite (i.e. of the tribe of Levi) brought the following (festal letter) about Purim, of which they said that it was (the correct one) and Lysimachus, the son of Ptolemaeus, of those in Jerusalem, translated it.[131]

The date on which it was brought is usually supposed to be 114 BCE. The whole matter is to be understood as a piece of Hasmonaean

propaganda among the Jews of Egypt, as indeed is also indicated in
II Macc.2.14f. The extended translation, with religious elaborations,
has an 'anti-Macedonian' character; in particular the royal documents
in the additions display a very mannered style. Probably here the
author made particular efforts over his style. And presumably by
sending out such propaganda documents from Jerusalem and elsewhere the Hasmonaeans also wanted to restrain the influence of the
rival Oniad temple in Leontopolis with its markedly Hellenized
priesthood. In all probability not only was the Hebrew book of Esther
translated into Greek in Jerusalem, but at the same time this was also
the scene of the composition of those xenophobic additions in which,
for example, the Agagite Haman was made into a Macedonian who
wanted to betray the Persian kingdom to the Macedonians (E 10-14).
It is also striking that the Greek of the additions is substantially better
than that of the translated passages: in particular the royal letters
match the ceremonious document style of the time (B 1-7; E 1-23).
The author seems to have taken particular care over the Greek of
these additions.

The translations of I Maccabees – a piece of Hasmonaean propaganda – and of Judith, Tobit, etc., may also very well have been made
in Palestine. The same thing is true of the Greek version of Chronicles,
the version of I Esdras with its novellistic additions and the later
renderings of II Esdras (Ezra and Nehemiah), the Song of Songs,
Lamentations and Koheleth. The last of these works was only
translated very late, at the beginning of the second century CE, wholly
in the linguistic style of the version by Aquila. However, it is no longer
possible with any certainty to discover where these late works were
translated.[132]

The grandson of Ben Sira, who according to the prologue emigrated
to Egypt in 132 BCE and who, as he found there 'the beginnings of a
not insignificant education',[133] made a very passable translation of his
grandfather's work into Greek in order to satisfy this 'hunger for
education', will have acquired his basic knowledge of Greek in
Jerusalem; he basically wrote as a propagandist for the Jewish-
Palestinian wisdom tradition.

We find the opposite possibility, that of a Diaspora Jew writing a
historical work on the basis of being a personal eyewitness of events
in Palestine, in Jason of Cyrene, whom I have already mentioned:
entirely in the style of the solemn and dramatic historiography of his
time he composed a highly rhetorical work in five books. These
covered the preliminary history of the Hellenistic reform in Jerusalem

and the first part of the Maccabaean revolt, up to around the death of Judas Maccabaeus in 161 BCE. Jason seems to have known Eupolemus, as he makes particular mention of him at a striking point of his book (II Macc.4.11).[134] Jason's knowledge of Jewish Palestinian warfare, geography and piety seems to be hardly less precise than that of Josephus.

Acts 24.1 indicates that there was advanced rhetorical training in Jerusalem towards the middle of the first century; it depicts how the high priest Ananias[135] came down from Jerusalem with some members of the Sanhedrin and the orator Tertullus to accuse Paul before Felix. The orator will hardly have earned most of his pay – like most of his colleagues in the Roman empire – simply by making speeches in trials; teaching will have been the main source of his income. Luke exercises all his stylistic skill in developing the speech in 24.2-8; the introduction to the speech is the finest Greek sentence in the New Testament. In so doing he wants to show that the Jewish leaders of the people spared no expense in their accusation against Paul, but brought a real expert with them.[136] Later the rabbis knew not only the loanwords ῥήτωρ and σοφιστής, but also numerous technical rhetorical terms from the legal sphere.[137]

These examples show that it is not so simple to distinguish between the 'Jewish-Hellenistic' literature of the Diaspora and the 'genuine Jewish' literature of Palestine. Almost all accounts of intertestamental Jewish literature suffer from their desire to make too simple a distinction here. There were connections in all directions, and a constant and lively interchange. Wacholder and others therefore consider that a whole series of 'Jewish Hellenistic' writings or writers who are usually placed in Alexandria came into being in, or originated in and were active in, the mother country of Palestine. The works they have in mind here are the Alexander legend which has been preserved in Josephus,[138] the Tobiad Romance, the fragments of Pseudo-Hecataeus,[139] the chronographer Demetrius,[140] the older Philo with his didactic poem on Jerusalem,[141] the Samaritan Theodotus with his praise of Shechem and the sons of Jacob,[142] and the tragedian Ezekiel.[143]

However, here basically we cannot get further than conjectures, and this possibility should not be exaggerated. A Palestinian origin seems to me to be most likely in the case of the epic poet Philo, who in hexameters praises the aqueducts of Jerusalem constructed by the Hasmonaeans, and to be probable in the case of Theodotus, whose didactic poem on Shechem, 'the holy city', contrasts with the Letter of Aristeas in presupposing a good knowledge of the place; it must have been written in the second century BCE. At least both authors seem to have known Jerusalem and Shechem respectively from personal acquaintance.[144] The distinctive feature of many of these writings is that in a way which shows great self-awareness they praise *Jewish* Palestine, its inhabitants and its tradition partly in typical Greek forms of literature. The Tobiad Romance (Josephus, *Antt.* 12.154-224, 228-238), both of whose heroes, Joseph and his son Hyrcanus, are Palestinian Jews, poses a particular problem. Here I would endorse Bickerman's verdict:

> The story of the Tobiads was obviously written in Palestine. Readers in Alexandria or Ascalon would hardly have been enthusiastic about a tax collector who cheated them. But Jerusalem was proud of these native sons who did so well and who, like other successful businessmen of the Hellenistic age, remembered their home towns.[145]

In that case here we would have probably the only direct literary testimony from the sphere of the Jewish Hellenists of the Maccabaean period which has come down to us. Josephus mentions it in his history because in it Jewish Palestinian aristocrats were the heroes and because he could use it to fill the great gap between Alexander and the Maccabaean period. Nevertheless, even after two hundred years he seems to take delight in this biographical narrative in the same way as Jewish aristocrats in the early Hellenistic period. Here it is again worth listening to Bickerman:

> The publication of the biography of the Tobiads shows that among the contemporaries of Ben Sira there were many in Jerusalem who not only read Greek but also appreciated a book, written to the Greek taste, one in which the only Jewish elements were the proper names of the heroes of the story.[146]

The same problem of the impossibility of making a sharp and clear-cut division between a 'Palestinian Jewish' literature and a 'Jewish Hellenistic' literature also applies to parts of the popular novellistic wisdom and apocalyptic writing; this was on quite a different level, which to the Greeks will have been 'barbarian'. The boundary between the original Greek literature of the Diaspora and the originally Aramaic and Hebrew 'Palestinian literature' is not as easy to draw as is generally assumed. Moreover the dispute as to whether a work was originally composed in Greek or in a Semitic language is sometimes insoluble. The investigation by Ulrich Fischer,[147] for example, reckons with the possibility that over and above the Additions to Esther those to Daniel and the Ezekiel Apocryphon were written in the Greek language in Palestine, and he thinks that 'both the original language and the place of origin' of a further number of apocalyptic works – the Zephaniah apocalypse which has come down to us in Coptic, the Testament of Abraham[148] and individual fragments (Eldad and Medad, the Elijah apocalypse) are 'completely uncertain'.[149] On the other hand he conjectures a Semitic original from the area of Palestine for works the original language of which is equally quite uncertain, as for example the *Paralipomena Jeremiae*, the Apocalypse of Moses (or the Life of Adam and Eve), the Old Slavonic Apocalypse of Abraham, the greater part of the *Vitae Prophetarum* and the fragments of Jannes and Jambres.[150] At least in the case of the *Vita Jeremiae*, however, an Egyptian origin is more probable, as the author himself concedes.[151] The place of origin of the Testaments of the Twelve Patriarchs, for which a Greek original is now usually posited, is also quite open. The Testaments of Judah and Levi have more of a 'Palestinian' stamp, and the Testament of Joseph has a markedly Egyptian character; however, this is also connected with the themes of the writing, and in addition has strong echoes of the Greek Phaedra legend in the version in Euripides' *Hippolytus*.[152] In the later tradition of the Testaments of the Twelve Patriarchs the influence of the Palestinian Aramaic Testament literature becomes evident.[153] Here too one cannot get very far with an abrupt division between Palestinian Judaism and Hellenistic Diaspora Judaism.

It is therefore often very difficult to attribute particular theological views predominantly or exclusively to '*the* Hellenistic Diaspora' or to 'Palestinian Judaism'. In the first place too little attention is paid to the fact that Greek-speaking Diaspora Judaism was even less a unity than the Judaism of Palestine before 70 CE, which, as we now know, was a very complex phenomenon. Furthermore we do not have very much literary evidence that (leaving aside the unique and fundamentally incomparable work of Philo) we can assign to this Diaspora Judaism which was so disparate in itself, if only for geographical and social reasons.[154] From the great Jewish community in Rome, which was substantially different from that in Alexandria, apart from a few pieces of information from Philo and Josephus, virtually all we have are epigraphic sources. Here it in particular had especially close ties with the mother country.[155] Moreover our knowledge about Jewish literature from Syrian Antioch – apart from

IV Maccabees, which probably comes from there – remains quite uncertain.

In addition, the pre-rabbinic writings which certainly or probably come from Palestinian Judaism and were originally composed in Aramaic or Hebrew have only come down to us by being translated into Greek – in Palestine or outside it; who knows? – and were taken over by the Christian tradition. The only exceptions here are the newly-discovered original texts from Qumran and their 'forerunners' from the Cairo Geniza: the Damascus Document and the fragments of Sirach. The writings which are given the very vague designation 'Apocrypha and Pseudepigrapha' have all been handed down by the Christian church.[156] They for their part influenced the Diaspora, and later Christianity, just as conversely the literature of Diaspora Judaism was also read in Palestine. All this shows that with our usual stereotyped conceptions and labels we are no longer capable of doing justice to the complicated historical reality of Judaism in antiquity, and often do it violence instead.

All in all, I would suppose that as the metropolis of Jewish Palestine between the Maccabaean period and its destruction, Jerusalem had a far greater spiritual influence within the Jewish Diaspora in the east and in the west than Jewish Alexandria, and that (leaving aside Philo's *magnum opus*) the extent of its literary production was greater than that of the Jews in Alexandria.

The view that basically only the rabbinic Judaism that created a broad foundation of sources in Hebrew and Aramaic in the form of the Talmudic literature, the Midrashim and Targumim, might be designated 'Palestinian Judaism' in the full sense of the word and that everything else, including the Pseudepigrapha, indeed ultimately even the Qumran literature, can be praised or dismissed – depending on one's standpoint – as Hellenistic, is particularly pernicious. This view, which for example Gressmann put forward in his argument with Moore, but which still can be found today,[157] makes the confusion complete. In fact the multiform 'Hellenistic' influence on the rabbis is manifest,[158] and the early Pharisees were evidently more open to their 'Hellenistic' environment than the rigoristic Essenes. They also travelled abroad more frequently (Matt.23.15), though before 70 there is no evidence of any Pharisaic schools outside Jewish Palestine. Rather, we must try to pass an individual judgment on the geographical origin and theological and cultural context of each single text and each single author, at the same time also taking note of the problem of the author's social position and educational level.

4

The Political and Social Aspects of 'Hellenization'

The pressure to accept the superior 'Hellenistic world civilization' came from outside; it was a matter of political, economic, cultural and spiritual self-preservation. It was necessary to get to grips with the Greek spirit which apparently dominated the world in so many areas, by learning as much as possible from it. Therefore the ruling classes, including the clear-sighted rulers and popular leaders – right up to Jehuda han-nasi' and the Jewish patriarchs – were interested in Greek education, and even where everything foreign was abruptly rejected, as for example among the Essenes,[159] people were influenced by the new spirit without noticing the fact. The main hindrance here – as in antiquity generally – was the limited range of social education. 'The man who guides the plough' or wields the 'ox-goad' had no time to acquire an education, Greek or even Jewish (Sir.38.24ff.).[160] Hillel, the immigrant from Babylon and day worker,[161] who virtually forced his way into school, was an exception, and at the same time the symbol of a new development for which the Pharisees were responsible: in contrast to the crowns of priests and kings, 'the crown of the Torah' is potentially there for *all*;[162] their aim was to train the whole people in the law.[163]

The Hasmonaean high priests and later kings already had to recognize that for reasons of state they could not dispense with Greek technology, economics, law and warfare, language. So the Jewish expansion took place in Samaria, the coastal region, Galilee and Transjordan as in the Hellenistic monarchies, among other things by the foundation of Jewish military colonies. Later, for example in Galilee, these formed the main bases in the fight against Herod and the Romans.[164] According to *Antiquities* 13.318, in his short reign of little more than a year Aristobulus I adopted the popular surname

'Philhellene' which was popular among eastern monarchs (see above, p.8), possibly along with the title of king; his brother and successor Alexander Jannaeus not only had coins minted with Greek inscriptions[165] but also hired mercenaries from Asia Minor to preserve and extend his power. His foreign and domestic policies, his life-style and style of government, largely corresponded to that of other Hellenistic and eastern rulers, like that of the successful Mithridates VI of Pontus or the Armenian, Parthian and Nabataean kings. Hardly had the high priest Simon, the last of the five Maccabaean brothers, who achieved independence in 141 after a twenty-six year struggle, come to power than he built a mausoleum completely in the Hellenistic style of his time in honour of his father Mattathias and his hero brothers.[166] The edifice was so tall that it could be seen from the sea.[167] This monument consisted of seven pyramid tombs and 'pillars with weapons', probably trophies; this was a usual element of Hellenistic architecture and thus was completely secular in character.[168] The same is true of the poetic eulogy over Simon in I Macc.14.4-14, despite its imitation of the language of the Old Testament:[169] the name of God no longer appears, but only praise of Simon's good and heroic actions. Leaving aside the linguistic garb – it was originally written in Hebrew – it belongs in the genre of the typical Hellenistic encomium. If we compare it with the poetic eulogy by Ben Sira on the high priest Simon the Just (50.1-21) about two generations earlier, though of course this has a very much more marked religious stamp, it becomes clear that the path towards 'Hellenistic secularization' could no longer be blocked, despite the successful Maccabaean revolt.

The way in which I Maccabees 1.41f. bases the narrative of the persecution proper on the historically questionable command of King Antiochus IV to all his kingdom 'that all should be one people and that each should give up his customs (νόμιμα)' recalls the Hasmonaean policy of Judaizing under Hyrcanus and his successors which compelled the Idumaeans and later the Ituraeans in Galilee to adopt the Jewish law,[170] i.e. at a time when the 'chronicle of Maccabaean heroes', I Maccabees, was written. Underlying this conduct, which was unusual in antiquity, is on the one hand the theocratic conception of the purity of the land, which was sullied by uncircumcised idolaters, and alongside it also the secular conception of the economic and cultural (which to Jewish eyes at the same time meant religious) unity of the Hellenistic state. It was encountered above all in the Ptolemaic empire or in Pergamon, and Antiochus IV also kept it as the aim of his efforts.[171]

At that time the Hasmonaeans took part in profitable piracy in the eastern Mediterranean from the port of Joppa, which had already been captured by Simon.[172] The tomb of the Jewish aristocrat Jason, who had presumably been a successful pirate captain, contains Greek graffiti which with their motto 'Rejoice as long as you live' have a quite Epicurean ring,[173] and illustrate the new Hellenistic aristocratic lifestyle which was already known to Koheleth around 150 years earlier:

> Bread is made for laughter, and wine gladdens life, and money answers everything (10.19).

E.Bickerman makes a sarcastic comment on the relationship between the old aristocracy and the new:

> The arrogant aristocracy spoken of by Kohelet and Ben Sira was swept away by the Maccabean tempest because of its unorthodoxy. (The new leaders were no less rapacious, but more godly.)[174]

But things did not go too well even with 'godliness' and 'orthodoxy' in the new Hasmonaean ruling house and its military nobility. The embittered protest of the Psalms of Solomon and the Pesharim of Qumran speak for themselves here, and the same is true of the rebellion of the Pharisees which broke out during the reign of Alexander Jannaeus.

Presumably Jason was a Sadducee, i.e. a member of that new party of the priestly upper class which Josephus compares with the Epicureans. The loanword *'appīqōrōs* appears in the Mishnah as a designation for the Jew who despises the law and is a freethinker,[175] and rabbinic legend reports that when 'King Jannai' parted company with the Pharisees and joined the Sadducees, *'appīqōrsūt* had entered into him.[176] Another rabbinic legend connects the civil war between the sons of Jannai, which is said to have led to the desecration of the Temple, with the ominous effect of the *hokmat yᵉwanīt*, Greek wisdom, which thereafter is said to have been prohibited in Israel. This prohibition, which is repeated almost as a stereotype in connection with later catastrophes, is a sign that if there were such limitations, in the end they remained ineffective, since the ruling class never observed them.[177] And later, when after the catastrophe of 70 CE the Pharisees had taken over the spiritual leadership of the people, the most important family, the dynasty of Hillel from which the later patriarchs were descended, continued to be indebted to Greek education.[178]

In essence Herod merely developed consistently a tendency which was already visible among the Hasmonaeans, but in a new situation, i.e. in a form appropriate to the rule of the Roman principate. He saw himself in absolutely every respect as a Hellenistic ruler.[179] Certainly he was also a cruel tyrant, but his rages were no worse than those of other Hellenistic oriental potentates of his time (like Alexander Jannaeus) and his terrorism was not primarily the emanation of personal cruelty but served to preserve his power, which was under constant threat. In what follows we are not interested in a moral judgment which – as in the case of most of the eastern rulers who were his contemporaries – must be overwhelmingly negative, but in the cultural aspect of his reign. Even now it is extraordinarily difficult to get a clear picture of him, because in the *Antiquities*, which are our main source, Josephus bases himself on two downright contradictory sources: on the king's closest friend, Nicolaus of Damascus, and on a resolutely anti-Herodian priestly source[180] – a further example of priestly historiography in Greek in Jewish Palestine. The negative statement in *Antt.* 19.329 that 'Herod was far more friendly towards the Greeks than towards the Jews', especially as he honoured 'the cities of the foreigners' with a wealth of expensive buildings and gifts, while 'he did not think any Jewish city worth even a slight improvement or gift', does not correspond in this form to historical truth. As I have indicated above, Herod made Jerusalem a pearl among the cities of the Roman empire, and in Jewish territory he built not only palaces like Jericho[181] and Masada[182], and a great palace complex with a fortress at Bethlehem, Herodium, in which he was buried,[183] but also – and Josephus says nothing about this – the tomb of the patriarchs in Hebron[184] and a memorial in honour of Abraham and Isaac in Mamre.[185] Of the cities which he founded with a predominantly Jewish(-Samaritan) population, mention might be made of Antipatris in the plain of Sharon and Phasaelis in the Jordan valley north of Jericho;[186] the former Phoenician foundation which was once called Strato's Tower, refounded as Caesarea Sebaste,[187] also had a very large Jewish (and Samaritan) element in its population (see above, 14). Outwardly, Herod's Jerusalem was a Hellenistic city through and through, which had been decked in splendour as a result of the king's ambition (see above, 12f.). It contained a theatre and a hippodrome, as did the winter residence of Jericho.[188] The archaeological excavators have given an admirable description of this last:

> Everything about this civic centre instantly calls up Rome and Pompeii. Indeed, one may say that here in New Testament Jericho

is a section of Augustan Rome that has been miraculously trans-
ported on a magic carpet from the banks of the Tiber to the banks
of the Wadi Qelt.[189]

The technical and artistic level of the buildings was on a par with
that of the capitals of its day and in Rome was surpassed only two
generations later by Nero's passion for splendour. The king must have
imported a host of Greek and Roman architects and artists for
them, and also instructed native inhabitants in the art of Hellenistic
monumental architecture – even priests for the rebuilding of the
temple proper. We cannot exclude the possibility that the τέκτων
Jesus of Nazareth, son of the τέκτων Joseph, will have known more
about building than just how to construct simple Palestinian peasant
housing.

The simple poverty of the Essene building at Qumran is in deliberate
contrast to this luxurious construction, though in their artificial water
supply the Essenes were not willing to dispense with the most recent
technological achievements.[190] It was inevitable that the ruler by
Rome's grace should have shown what seemed appropriate reverence
to the Princeps and his cult by founding cities in Caesarea and Sebaste
which were in fact older Hellenistic cities (Strato's Tower and
Samaria) refounded and enlarged, a course of action for which he also
had political, economic and military reasons, and by building temples
to Augustus and Roma. Herod had to direct his policy towards
Augustus, to whom he owed everything. But on the other hand to an
amazing degree he also took note of the religious characteristics of the
Jewish population, which had been marked since the Maccabaean
period. Though the coins now had exclusively Greek inscriptions,
they did not bear the image of the ruler but harmless symbols,
sometimes neutral and sometimes religious.[191] It was only the flexible
Agrippa I, so popular everywhere because of his alleged piety, but in
reality just capable of adapting to anything, who dared to depart from
this practice.[192] Before him Herod's son Philip had already had coins
minted with the image of the emperor in Gaulanitis, Trachonitis and
Batanaea, but his territory did not have such an intensive Jewish
population as Judaea or Galilee. Moreover, so far no pictorial representations of human beings or animals have been found on the wall
paintings at Masada or Herodium which could be compared, say,
with the *trompes d'oeuil* on the estate of Livia in Primaporta.

In the territory really inhabited only by Jews there was neither
emperor worship nor alien cults, nor were there human represen-

tations in the form of statues and pictures – as would have been quite natural in a Greek city. Geometrical ornamentation, or ornamentation with plans and flowers, is quite predominant.[193] The rebuilding of the temple, behind which, as Shalit has shown,[194] lay a piece of political theology, earned Herod the praise of Jewish people all over the world. It made him to some extent Solomon *redivivus* and the prince of peace, since with God's blessing he had succeeded in doing what his Hasmonaean predecessors had proved unable to do. At the beginning of the speech with which Josephus (or Nicolaus) has the reason for the building of the temple given to the people, the monarch stresses that he has 'with God's will brought the Jewish people to a hitherto unprecedented state of prosperity':

> But since, by the will of God, I am now ruler and there continues to be a long period of peace and an abundance of wealth and great revenues, and – what is of most importance – the Romans who are, so to speak, the masters of the world, are (my) loyal friends, I will try to remedy the oversight caused by the necessity and subjection of the earlier time, and by this act of piety make full return to God for the gift of this kingdom.[195]

The warning inscriptions in Greek in the temple, which threaten the death penalty on all non-Jews, including Roman citizens, who enter the inner precincts of the temple, are also a sign of this consideration for Jewish piety.[196]

The king, who had already received a solid Greek education in the Jerusalem of the high priest Hyrcanus II, was particularly interested in higher Greek studies. He therefore brought one of the most significant scholars of his time, the Peripatetic Nicolaus of Damascus, to his court.[197] Nicolaus came from a prominent and educated family in the old Syrian capital.[198] The names of his father (Antipater) and mother (Stratonice) are typically Macedonian, but they were probably Hellenized Aramaeans. Herod's father, a Judaizing Idumaean aristocrat, bore the same name. As a trained public orator his father had had an important role during the turbulent years after the collapse of the Seleucid empire. Nicolaus was born about the time that Pompey ordered affairs in Syria (64 BCE). In his autobiography he gives his age after Herod's death (4 BCE) as about sixty. He seems to have had an excellent education in Damascus, all his life felt himself to be a Greek and at the same time to have a close bond with Roman rule since this was the patron of Greek culture in Syria. As a scholar he had extensive knowledge and many skills; among other things he will

have composed tragedies and comedies, and occupied himself with
music and mathematics. Philosophically he considered himself an
'Aristotelian', i.e. a scholar of encyclopaedic learning. At the heart of
his scholarly activity, however, was his polished rhetorical historiography. Thanks to his manifold gifts, which developed early, a
glittering career opened up to him.

Initially Nicolaus became the teacher of Antony and Cleopatra's
children, but before 20 BCE Herod got to know him better and
brought him to his court. He remained the king's adviser and friend
until Herod's death in 4 BCE. On the king's prompting and for his
own use he wrote a world history in 144 books, substantial parts of
which were composed in Jerusalem; Josephus copied out from it the
passages about the Jews. His picture of early Jewish history must
have been interesting; among other things he makes Abraham king
of Damascus before he comes to Palestine.[199] Another work dedicated
to Herod discussed the customs of the peoples, and Nicolaus's
biography of Augustus falls in the period of his association with the
king. Nicolaus also instructed his royal pupil in philosophy, rhetoric
and history; the ruler, who was quick to learn, really liked only the
two latter disciplines and allowed Nicolaus to persuade him to write
his memoirs – certainly in Greek – which Nicolaus probably again
used for his history.[200] It was natural for Herod to entrust the education
of his younger sons to this man of letters (in the best sense of the term),
an education which was then continued in Rome. In addition two
further 'friends' of Herod are mentioned, Andromachus and Gemellus,
who also functioned as ambassadors and political counsellors. They
'supported him in the instruction of his sons' or had their own sons
'educated (with his)' but then fell out of favour (*Antt.* 16.242f.).

The tradition of higher education was continued in the family with
Herod's grandsons – mention should be made here primarily of King
Agrippa I – and great-grandsons. So Josephus can say to Agrippa II
that he and his relations were 'men who had received a thorough
Greek education' (*Vita* 359). Given the king's zeal for learning,
Jerusalem must have had a good Greek library; this is also presupposed
by the wide-ranging literary works of Nicolaus and the cultivation of
the theatre. The royal library was on a par with that of the temple.[201]
The very different library of Qumran with around a thousand scrolls
gives us a vivid idea of the extent of such libraries. In both contexts
'education' stood high – though in quite a different sense. In addition
to Nicolaus, numerous other Greeks lived at the royal court: scholars,
technicians, artists, politicians, soldiers and also adventurers – one

might call them parasites. This cultural policy of the king was probably not just a royal whim, but was shared by other client kings. It was an old tradition that eastern kings called themselves 'Philhellene', friend of the Greeks (and later also *philoromaios*, friend of the Romans). We find this among the Parthians, the Nabataeans, in Armenia, Cappadocia and Commagene (see above, p.8). Herod therefore could not lag behind. Moreover he had the ambitious aim of integrating the disputatious Jews into the ecumene of the Roman empire. We may assume that this concern for education had an influence on the aristocratic circles of Jerusalem, indeed throughout the whole country. Anyone who wanted to be anyone at the court in Jerusalem and among the ruling class there had to speak Greek and have at least the beginnings of 'Greek education'. Here Herod did not want to lag behind his neighbours. Wacholder lists more than forty authors, especially historians – to be inferred from the works of Nicolaus – who may have been in Herod's library. In this environment, which certainly advanced beyond the royal palace, even a scribe like Hillel may have been influenced by the Greek spirit: 'Certainly the leading Pharisees studied Greek, even when they attempted to discourage its dissemination among the people.'[202]

These efforts were backed up by the king's efforts over the Greek-speaking Diaspora. He regarded himself as its patron and it strengthened his influence in the Roman empire. In the eyes of the Greeks and Romans Herod seemed, by contrast, to be an exotic oriental, but at the same time also a Jew who observed the law and represented the interests of his people. A Greek writer, Ptolemaeus, possibly a contemporary from Ashkelon, wrote a biography of King Herod. The numerous references to Herod in ancient writers demonstrate some interest in his person and subjects.[203] Here one could speak of a new ἀκμή τις Ἑλληνισμοῦ, a climax of Hellenism which is in some respects comparable to that after 175 BCE, though it differed from the latter in no longer representing any real danger to the Jewish faith. The king could not shake the strict monotheism of his people, bound to the Torah, which for all his 'liberalism' he himself shared, nor did he want to. His significance and his reputation as a ruler were at the same time bound up with the national and religious identity of Judaism in the mother country. As the king kept firm control of the land from the capture of Jerusalem in 37 BCE until his death, during those thirty-three years he will have left a more than superficial stamp on it in cultural and political terms also, which will have gone deeper and reached wider strata of the population. Had the Romans left the dynasty which Herod founded in power – above all after the death of Agrippa I, who was also a grandson of Herod's Hasmonaean wife Mariamne – and had the slow Hellenization of the upper classes continued in Jerusalem, the radicals would not have got the upper hand and the city would not have been destroyed.

Some protests, like the destruction of the golden eagle on the Temple[204] and the revolts after the king's death, in which a former slave of the ruler plundered and burned down the villas and palaces in the Jordan valley, and a former shepherd emerged with messianic claims,[205] show a similar 'anti-Hellenistic' reaction among ordinary people to that at the time of the Maccabean revolt. However, since the foundations of Jewish belief were not threatened, so that the protests did not find any widespread response among all classes of the people and enjoyed only modest political success, the process of Hellenization continued.

That this not only affected the 'first families' but even did not leave the moderate wing of the opposition, the pious, untouched, is shown by the example of Hillel, the greatest Pharisaic teacher before 70 CE, whom Leo Baeck called 'the secret anti-king against Herod',[206] and who became the leader of the 'liberals' within the Pharisaic party. True, we only have comparatively little information about him, the historicity of which can be verified; however, some of the traditions relating to him have a marked Hellenistic stamp. This tendency continued to be a determining factor for the family of the patriarch, which was a leading spiritual and political influence later, after the great catastrophes of 66-70 and 132-135.[207]

The sons of Herod further developed the 'cultural policy' inspired by the ideal of the Hellenistic ruler, since their political prestige in the Roman empire was also connected with the splendour of the 'enlightened despotism' of their rule. This is more evident in the case of Philip the tetrarch and above all of Herod Antipas, ruler of the territory in which Jesus lived, than in the case of Archelaus, of whom we know hardly anything, since as early as 6 CE he was banished to Gaul for maladministration. In particular the cities founded by Philip, which I have already mentioned, are striking.

First of all he rebuilt Sepphoris (about four miles north of Nazareth, see p.17 above), which had been destroyed by Varus in 4 BCE, and gave it the name 'Autocratoris' (*Antt.* 18.27). The almost exclusively Jewish population resolutely took the side of the Romans in the Jewish revolt, an attitude which probably derives not only from their bitter experiences in the year 4 BCE but also from the greater 'degree of

Hellenization' of the city and its long role as the capital of Galilee. Josephus calls it the 'jewel of all Galilee' (ibid.). The inhabitants seem to have learned their lesson from the destruction of the city in 4 BCE. Probably because it kept the peace with Rome the city was given the new name 'Eirenopolis' (and 'Neronias'). In the course of his anti-Jewish policy Hadrian then called it Diocaesarea. When Nero bestowed Tiberias and its territory on King Agrippa II (in 61?), Sepphoris again became the capital of Galilee. Possibly it was already at that time that the city was named 'Neronias', while the title 'Eirenopolis' was bestowed on it soon afterwards, because of its conduct in the Jewish war.

In Peraea Antipas changed the old 'Betharamphta' into a new foundation in honour of the empress Livia (at first Livias and after 14 CE Julias).[208] However, his most significant new foundation was his new residence of Tiberias, which was presumably laid out in 17–20 CE. As the city had been erected over graves, it is said to have been initially avoided by Jews of a stricter observance.[209] Because of the difficulty of finding suitable inhabitants, the tetrarch resorted to compulsory settlement and in this way produced a population which was mixed socially and in terms of education, but was quite predominantly Jewish. The layout, planned in the usual Hippodamian form with streets running into one another at right angles, was dominated by the royal palace which, because it had representations of animals on it, was burnt down by the ordinary members of the population in 66, the first year of the revolt.[210] There would also have had to have been a theatre and a stadium. On the other hand, the ruler built the largest synagogue in Palestine, presumably modelled on the famous synagogue in Alexandria, the 'Diplostoon' with five naves.[211] In this respect, too, Antipas wanted to imitate his father, and as he could not build a second temple, his only possibility was to copy the greatest synagogue of his time.[212] He allowed the city to mint its own coins and have a Greek constitution with a *boule* headed by an *archon*. The administration of the city was further supervised by two officials of the tetrarch, a police officer (ὕπαρχος) and the overseer of the market (ἀγορανόμος). Claudius seems further to have extended the privileges of the city founded under Tiberius, since under Trajan and Hadrian the citizens designated themselves on coins as ΤΙΒΕΡΙΕΙΣ ΚΛΑΥΔΙΕΙΣ.[213]

At the beginning of the Jewish War the Hellenized upper class led by Justus and his father Pistus (*Vita* 390) sought to ward off both the rebels and attacks from the cities of the Decapolis. In other words, like the Jerusalem aristocracy it adopted a mediating attitude – in which it was no more successful than they were. The city fell into the hands of the rebels and then later had to pay for its involvement in the rebellion.

Evidently in Jewish Palestine to some degree Greek education, membership of the upper class and loyalty to Rome went together. Whereas in Sepphoris a theatre was excavated which held around 4-5000 people and was presumably built by Antipas (see p.74 n.90 below), Josephus (*BJ* 2.619f.; 3.538f.; *Vita* 92) and the Jerusalem Talmud (jEr 5.1 22b line 58) attest a great stadium in Tiberias. It seems probable that Antipas also built a theatre there. Tarichaea (Magdala) about three miles north of that had a hippodrome (*BJ* 2, 599; *Vita* 132f.) which was even larger than the stadium in Tiberias itself. These buildings served not only for the staging of games and recitations but also for popular assemblies.[214]

Thus the tendency to demonstrate one's superior status by knowledge of Greek and a degree of Greek education and customs continued under the sons of Herod, the Roman prefects and procurators, even if they no longer practised an 'offensive cultural policy' as the ambitious king had done. Presumably the 'Herodians', i.e. the members of Herod's wider family along with their political and economic clientèle in the broadest sense, were also well disposed to such attempts at education. Since these attempts were no longer associated with the denial of Jewish faith as in the time of Antiochus IV but had the attraction of economic advantages and better contacts with the Jews of the Diaspora and with leading officials and ministers, at least in the cities there will have been a substantial trend towards an elementary Greek education. However, a higher degree of literary studies as in the case, say, of Justus of Tiberias, remained the exception and was limited to a few individuals. An intellectual and volatile ruler like king Herod Agrippa I combined an ostentatious Jewish piety with a wholly liberal attitude – for example in the minting of coins and the divine worship of his person outside Jewish territory – in an amazing way.[215]

Only through the failure of the Roman procurators and their administration in the 50s did the radical anti-Roman forces, which were at the same time 'anti-Hellenistic', gain ground; in particular they could enlist the ordinary population of the country, and this put the more or less 'Hellenized' aristocracy in the cities, particularly in Jerusalem, in an increasingly difficult position.[216] In Caesarea, for example, a rich tax farmer named John, presumably also a banker –

comparable to the alabarch Alexander (Philo's brother) in Alexandria – was the political leader of the substantial Jewish group which called for the same political rights as the 'Greeks'.[217] Nero rejected this demand for *isopoliteia*, as did Claudius in his famous letter to the people of Alexandria, although the Jews in Caesarea were hardly less 'Hellenized' than those in the Egyptian metropolis. In so doing he planted the seeds of the Jewish rebellion, which basically broke out because part of the upper classes, disillusioned by Roman misrule and party politics, half-heartedly turned towards the radical groups of rebels, from whom they were far removed by education and social interests. For example in the first months of the crisis year the last procurator, Gessius Florus, had two prominent Jews, who had Roman citizenship and – presumably because of their substantial means – were, like Florus himself, both members of the *equites*, publicly scourged and crucified in Jerusalem against all Roman law.[218] These seem to have been Jews from Jerusalem (or Caesarea) who belonged to the uppermost level of society, those very circles from which John the tax farmer came. Possibly he was one of them. Despite these attacks, which above all affected the Hellenistic upper class, the majority of the Jerusalem aristocracy held out against the seizure of power by the radicals right to the end.

The rift which ran through the people was thus social, educational and cultural at the same time. Despite the attempts at mediation by Agrippa II and his sister Berenice (who later became Titus's mistress), in alliance with leading priests and liberal Pharisees, disaster could no longer be staved off. The attempt by Herod and his successors to integrate Judaea into the Roman empire by encouraging Greek education among the 'upper ten thousand' was doomed to failure.

The fearful catastrophe of the First Jewish War in 66-70 CE violently destroyed an independent and flourishing Jewish-Hellenistic culture, involving a not inconsiderable part of the population, which had its own stamp, differing from that of the Jewish centres of the Diaspora: Alexandria, Antioch, Rome, Cyrene or the cities of Asia Minor. This special Jewish-Hellenistic culture of the Judaean metropolis was as it were 'decapitated' by the break-away from Rome, which was disastrous in every respect, and led to terrible consequences. This Jewish-Hellenistic culture in the capital itself had an amazing multiplicity, corresponding to the social and cultural pluralism of the Jerusalem population before 70. The circles which gave it support included the far-flung clan of Herod and his clientèle, the 'Herodians', the leading high-priestly families, the numerous people who returned from the Diaspora including well-to-do proselytes who gathered in synagogue communities corresponding to their countries of origin, rich landowners, merchants, 'manufacturers' who did excellent business in this the greatest pilgrimage city of the empire, not to mention all those who through status and profession had to collaborate closely with the Roman powers. These circles, which were not united among themselves and sometimes were hopelessly divided in political terms, for a long time joined the moderate Pharisees of the Hillel school and the whole of the Jerusalem middle class in offering successful resistance to the Jewish revolutionaries, who increasingly dominated the open country, though it was no longer possible to ward off disaster.[219]

The attitude of the earliest Christian community in this spiritual and social conflict was a divided one. The principle was that where God's reign was dawning, questions of social prestige, alien civilization and education had to lose their significance completely. The Jesus movement and the earliest community were very different from secular 'educational movements'. At the same time Jesus – and the earliest community – clearly distanced himself not only from the luxury and alien lifestyle of the Herodian rulers and the claims to power of the first families but also from the nationalistic zeal of the radicals. However, this whole political and social area is only a marginal theme in the proclamation of Jesus and his movement.

With exemplary method Gerd Theissen has been able to interpret Matthew 11.7f./Luke 7.25f. as specific polemic against Antipas and as support for the circle of John the Baptist by using coins minted at the foundation of Tiberias and the reed depicted on them. From his interpretation of this logion in terms of contemporary history it becomes clear how in all probability we can identify an authentic saying of Jesus here. As Antipas was banished to Gaul as early as 38 CE, this saying with its unique parallelism between a 'reed moved by the wind' and 'a man in soft raiment', 'gorgeously apparelled and living in luxury in kings' courts', certainly cannot be a late 'community construction'. It would only be comprehensible to the immediate contemporaries of Jesus and John the Baptist, but nevertheless has been handed down relatively unchanged. The derogatory designation of Antipas as an ever-adaptable 'reed' also matches the title 'fox' given to him in Luke 13.32.[220] However, we have no parallel with Jesus to John the Baptist's specific criticism of Antipas's marriage arrangements, which corresponded to the alien lifestyle of, for example, the Roman aristocracy. Certainly, like the Letter of James later, he criticized the rich who lived 'all their days splendidly and in joy', but he also gained followers specifically from the educated middle and upper class, and received financial support from leading ladies, for example Johanna, wife of Herod's steward (ἐπίτροπος = *procurator*)[221] Chuza (Luke 8.3). This in turn led to his being reviled by the other side, the representatives of radical piety, as a 'glutton and winebibber' (Matt.11.19).

The 'Hellenized' cities like Tiberias and Sepphoris play no part in the Gospels.[222] Tiberias appears only in the Gospel of John, which was written from a Jerusalem standpoint and sometimes has an almost aristocratic character.[223] Outside Galilee, too, according to Mark Jesus visits only the 'regions of Tyre and Sidon' lying outside the real *poleis* and 'the villages (of the territory) of Caesarea Philippi',[224] the city founded by Philip as capital of his tetrarchy in place of the older Panias. According to the place names in the Gospels, Jesus avoided the larger cities – apart from Jerusalem, where he was executed (Luke 13.33). Yet within two decades primitive Christianity became markedly a city religion.[225] The members of the earliest Christian community called themselves 'the poor',[226] yet they were grateful for the well-to-do families who owned houses (Acts 2.46; 9.36-39; 14.14f.). What was fatal for Jesus was his clash with the Sadducean priestly nobility in the Jewish capital, who because of his messianic claim handed him over to Pilate and also persecuted the later community with its hatred to the point of executing James the brother of Jesus and other Jewish Christians in 62 CE. In those circles there was fear of the 'subversive' power of the new message, fear that it could endanger the unstable *status quo*. By contrast it is striking that we do not hear anything of a persecution by the Roman authorities in Palestine before the time of Domitian and Trajan. The procurator Albinus reacted very sharply to the execution of James and the other Jewish Christians by the high priest Annas II (Josephus, *Antt.* 20.200f.).

What was decisive for the subsequent course of primitive Christianity, however, was the amazingly rapid and intensive effect of the new message on the Greek-speaking Hellenists[227] in Jerusalem and the proclamation of the message of Jesus beyond the bounds of Israel which began as early as the 30s as a result of this. Here we have that social stratum in Jerusalem the significance of which for the development of the city before 70 and here again particularly for the rise of the earliest community in the Jewish metropolis has so far been too neglected. The circle of Christians who came from it cannot have been all that small, otherwise their missionary activity in Jerusalem would not have provoked so much of a stir and caused such offence. The fact that these Hellenists in particular accepted the new messianic eschatological message and continued to develop its form in a creative way probably indicates an intrinsic affinity to the Hellenistic world along with a universality which was already concealed in Jesus' proclamation and activity. The relationship of the proclamation of Jesus and the synoptic tradition to Greek gnomic wisdom and to philosophical anecdotes (here above all Cynic anecdotes) still needs thorough investigation. Why should not the craftsman Jesus, who grew up in the neighbourhood of Sepphoris, have made contact with Cynic itinerant preachers, especially as he himself spoke some Greek? Only recently has this somewhat neglected point in the earliest history of Christianity been investigated more thoroughly in various studies by F.G.Downing. These affinities between Gospel tradition and Cynic religious and social criticism go right back to Jesus himself.[228]

5

'Hellenistic' Traditions in Jewish Palestine

If 'Greek education' in Jewish Palestine in the first century CE already had a tradition going back over centuries, then it should be possible also to demonstrate traces of it in that literature which was composed in a Semitic language and which was critical of the new spirit. However, methodologically it is very difficult to demonstrate whether here we have literary dependence or oral tradition, clear echoes or, rather, fortuitous analogies which are based on the convergence of oriental and Greek mythology in the Hellenistic period. We must also remember old ties between Greek myths and those of the ancient Near East which can already be demonstrated in Homer and Hesiod. Only exceptionally will Jewish apocalyptists have read Hellenistic secular literature – as in the case of the learned forgers of the Sibylline Oracles, and that was written primarily in Alexandria. On the other hand the mother‑country and the Holy City play a major role particularly in the Jewish Sibyllines, and one could suppose that at least one fragment (2.63-92), in which the coming of Beliar, the eschatological enemy of God, is depicted from the 'Sebastenes', i.e. probably from Samaria, was written in Jewish Palestine.[229]

That makes all the more significant the common 'religious *koine*' of the time (one could also say the 'religious spirit of the age') which is what made it possible for the eschatological-messianic message to be understood so easily by Greeks and Romans.[230] In what follows I can touch only briefly on this whole complex, which calls for a whole series of detailed monographs, especially as numerous works are being produced on it – including some by myself.[231]

In the Book of Daniel we come across the motive of the four successive world empires, deteriorating in quality, which we often find in ancient historians. Perhaps it is already of Persian origin; it is in turn associated with the series of four ages characterized by metals of diminishing worth which we again know from Hesiod.[232] Other 'Hellenistic' features are the astrological association of world empires with a sign of the zodiac (Daniel 8 and 9) and the metaphor of astral immortality in Daniel 12.1ff.[233]

In connection with future hope for the individual going beyond death which clearly emerges for the first time for martyrs in Dan.12 we must also remember that places of punishment for the godless in the underworld are an old Greek notion, and that in the earliest testimonies the resurrection does not yet have that massively realistic form which it takes on in the later Pharisaic haggada,[234] but still has a spiritualizing character similar to Paul's statement in I Cor.15.42-50. In the case of the few pieces of Essene evidence in this respect we must even ask whether Josephus was not right in attributing to the Essenes a doctrine of the immortality of the soul.[235] Perhaps – as also in earliest Christianity and in Pharisaism – both conceptions existed side by side. The contrast in principle which scholars are so fond of making between a Hellenistic-Jewish echatology of the rise of the soul to the heavenly world after death, orientated on the Greek conception of immortality, and an apocalyptic Palestinian hope of resurrection at the dawn of the kingdom of God imagined as taking place on earth, just does not exist in such an abrupt form. In the case of both Jesus and Paul and in the Johannine corpus the two conceptions stand side by side. They are in constant contact and can be demonstrated alongside each other and interwoven both in Jewish Palestine and in the Diaspora. There is no more an exclusive opposition here than there is between the earthly Messiah and a redeemer figure in the character of the Son of Man coming down from heaven.[236] Conversely the resurrection hope was certainly not just limited to Palestine: we also have a series of attestations of it from the Diaspora.[237] The transition to the hope for immortality was fluid and left different possibilities open. Here too the strict division between 'Hellenistic' Diaspora and motherland has not stood the test.

The 'mythological geography' of Ethiopian Enoch similarly has numerous points of contact with Greek ideas. This is true first of the kingdom of the dead in the distant West,[238] with a realm of light and a refreshing spring for the righteous. Here one thinks of the Elysian fields and the spring Mnemosyne; the stream of fire recalls the Pyriphlegeton and the dark places of punishment recall Tartarus. Possibly these conceptions go back to common myths shared by the Greeks and the Near East which now circulated more widely during the Hellenistic period in changed circumstances.[239] The utopian journey of Enoch into the fabulous lands beyond the Erythraean Sea, i.e. the Indian Ocean, which is said to be the location of paradise with its miraculous herbs (Ethiopian Enoch 30-32), recalls motives of the utopian travel romance.[240] No more needs to be said about the fact that the extensive descriptions of the journey into heaven which in the Testament of Levi for the first time leads through seven heavens[241] has numerous earlier Greek parallels;[242] from now on it is a stock item in both Hellenistic and Jewish revelation literature. Here German scholarship has wrongly constructed a fundamental difference between an allegedly apocalyptic temporal way of thinking which is determined by the contrast between the old aeon and the new and a Hellenistic or even Gnostic spatial way of thinking with the contrast between heavenly and earthly worlds.[243] Both were constantly related, particularly in apocalyptic.[244]

G.W.E.Nickelsburg sees the influence of the Greek Prometheus myth in the account of the rebellion and fall of the watchmen angels in Ethiopian Enoch 6-11,[245] whereas P.D.Hanson conjectures a common oriental source which for its part is said already to have influenced Hesiod.[246] The motive of the 'euhemeristic' hero and bringer of the cult which we find here and in the book of Jubilees may ultimately be of ancient Near Eastern origin, but it plays a major role in the Hellenistic world and is also regularly taken over by Judaism in its polemic against idolatry.[247] The notion that the souls of the giants who came into being as a result of the marriages of the fallen angels with human women became evil spirits, which emerges in Enoch and in Jubilees, also coincides completely with Greek demonology. In the same way the demonology of Judaism and early Christianity hardly has any demonstrably close connections with the Old Testament, where it is largely suppressed; however, it is all the more closely related to its Hellenistic/Near-Eastern environment.[248] Still, we have to reckon with the possibility that the earlier Old Testament tradition eliminated popular ideas about demons which were generally widespread (but cf. e.g. Deut.32.17 LXX and Paul in I Cor.10.20).

In an extended study I have discussed the 'Hellenistic' influences on the Essene movement.[249] I would see direct points of contact there in the military technique of the War Scroll, which is probably based on a Hellenistic handbook of tactics; the legal form of the private religious association;[250] the doctrine of two spirits which possibly derives from Alexandria but is ultimately Iranian; and above all in the horoscopes,[251] in which details of physiognomy are associated with astrological birth constellations. Astrology,[252] manticism and magic[253] played just as great a role in Judaism at the beginning of our era as they did in the pagan environment. The Temple Scroll with its markedly systematic features is also testimony to the rationalism of the Hellenistic period.[254] Just how complicated the problem of diffusion in the history of religion is emerges from the fact that it is precisely the Essenes, who were the bitterest opponents of all pagan, alien thought and knowledge, who seem particularly suited to be candidates for an *interpretatio graeca* not only by Jewish but also by pagan writers, and for a long time scholars regarded them as a group of Jewish neo-Pythagoreans, in some cases right up to the discovery of the Qumran texts.[255]

One could cite almost unlimited examples. In Ben Sira, who displays a series of unique points of contact with Stoicism, we find the first indication of the doctrine of two ways,[256] which in the form of the sign Y became the symbol of Pythagoreanism. Its best known literary expression is Prodicus' fable of Heracles at the crossroads in Xenophon.[257] Ben Sira also has the first beginnings of a doctrine of the *yēṣer*, which the rabbis then developed in the opposition of the 'good and evil inclination'.[258] This stands between Essene speculation on the two spirits[259] and Hellenistic anthropology with the distinction between the higher and lower power of the soul in human beings. There are also points of contact with philosophical controversies in the discussion of free will in the Jewish-Palestinian religious parties as they are depicted in Josephus.[260] Finally and in conclusion the theories of inspiration and forms of revelation in Hellenistic religions and Judaism are not all that different.[261] There are differentiations, some of which have a philological basis – for example, Jewish 'psychology' was not yet as developed as Greek – but despite these differences a variety of relationships was possible here. What unites the two is often greater than what separates them.

One fundamental feature which Jews and Greeks in the Hellenistic period had in common is the discovery of the religious individual and the individual's eschatological salvation disclosed quite personally through 'conversion', i.e. the hope of being able to pass over the boundary of death as individuals. Just as initiation into the mysteries, joining a *thiasos* of initiates or conversion to the philosophy which guarantees true life that corresponds to divine reason take place on the basis of the quite specific decisions of an individual, so similarly the Essenes summon individuals out of the *massa perditionis* of Israel to join the eschatological community of salvation of the 'true Israel', so John the Baptist preaches baptism on the Jordan as an eschatological sacrament and sign of true conversion, which can only be brought about by each individual, and Jesus calls on individuals to become disciples. Pharisaic emissaries 'travel over sea and land to gain *one* proselyte' (Matt.23.15); this could be an allusion to events like the conversion of King Izates. To use the language of Adolf von Harnack, while Jews and Greeks do not necessarily have the knowledge of 'God the Father'[262] in common, they do have in common a growing intimation of the 'infinite value of the human soul'.[263] At this point I would like to quote a lengthy passage from Harnack's second lecture on *What is Christianity?* which sets out the problem very clearly:

> The picture of Jesus' life and his discourses stand in no relation with the Greek spirit. That is almost a matter for surprise; for Galilee was full of Greeks, and Greek was then spoken in many of its cities... There were Greek teachers and philosophers there, and it is scarcely conceivable that Jesus should have been unacquainted with their language. But that he was in any way influenced by them, that he was ever in touch with the thoughts of Plato or the Stoa, even though it may have been only in some popular redaction, it is absolutely impossible to maintain. (*At this point, nowadays I would not be so certain*, M.H.) Of course if religious individualism – God and the soul, the soul and its God; if subjectivism; if the full self-responsibility of the individual; if the separation of the religious from the political – if all this is only Greek, then Jesus, too, stands within the sphere of Greek development; then he, too, breathed the pure air of Greece and drank from the Greek spring. But it cannot be proved that it is only on this one line, only in the Hellenic people, that this development took place... other nations also advanced to similar states of knowledge and feeling; although they did so, it is true, as a rule, only after Alexander the Great had pulled down the barriers and fences which separated the peoples. For these nations, too, no doubt it was in the majority of cases the Greek element that was the liberating and progressive factor. But I do not believe that the Psalmist who uttered the words, 'Whom have I in heaven but thee? and there is none upon earth that I desire beside thee,' had ever heard anything of Socrates and Plato.[264]

More important than 'influences' which are often hard to trace is the deep-rooted convergence in Old Testament-Jewish and Greek thought, for all the fundamental differences. It is already evident in

the manifold elements of the process of the Hellenization of Judaism
and in Christianity, the most fruitful synthesis that the ancient world
achieved. One may disagree with Harnack's remarks for many
reasons, but he is more correct than we would have it today:

> 'I say to you that there is more joy in heaven over *one* sinner who
> repents than over ninety-nine just persons who need no repentance'
> (Luke 15.7).

That is not addressed to the collective which is constantly so highly
praised today but addresses each individual as a sinner before God.
And Peter's answer in the name of the disciples (Mark 10.28, 'Behold,
we have left all and followed you') is the answer of those who become
individuals through Jesus' personal call before God and to whom as
a result the new community of the dawning kingdom of God is given.[265]

This point of the discovery of the individual before God is probably
the greatest gain of that encounter between the Jewish and Greek
spirits which was so influential and at the same time so passionate.
The certainty of the overcoming of death and the stress on the value
of the individual unite in the glorification of the martyr. The Old
Testament could not yet know the praise of the hero who dies for his
ancestral city and its gods, but we find this praise of heroes all the
more, say, in Greek poetry during the period of the Persian war.
Although there are many reports in ancient Israel of the death of
prophets and their faithfulness to YHWH, the prophets are never
transformed into martyrs: in contrast to Greece, in Israel before the
Hellenistic period (apart from the enigmatic text Isa.53) there is
never any mention of a heroic 'dying for' (ἀποθνήσκειν ὑπέρ).[266] That
changes at a stroke in the Maccabean period, and does so specifically
in the literature related to Palestine.[267] In the book of Daniel the three
young men in the burning fiery furnace (cf. Dan.3.28) appear as the
first martyrs who are saved in miraculous fashion, but even in this
first 'apocalypse' the persecution of the 'wise' serves as atonement for
their own sins. On the other hand, though, the martyrs are promised
a special reward (Dan.12.1-4). In I Macc.2.50 the dying Mattathias
calls on his sons to sacrifice their lives *for* the covenant of their fathers,
and in 6.44 his heroic son Eleazar sacrifices himself like the Greek
warriors in the Persian period 'to save his people and make for himself
an eternal name' – quite a new idea. II Maccabees 6 and 7 have the
first extended accounts of martyrdoms, and from now on the formulae
of 'dying for' God's law and the people he has chosen accumulate.[268]
Beginning with the Jewish exegesis of Genesis 22 and Isaiah 53, at

the same time the idea of the vicarious expiation in the death of the righteous also occurs increasingly. H.S.Versnel, who has provided the most exhaustive and convincing treatment of the problem, ends by remarking: 'Could the question "Greek" or "Jewish" possibly be answered here simplistically but more satisfyingly with "Hellenistic"?'[269]

There remains the mass of rabbinic traditions for us to investigate briefly, though these predominantly belong to a later period. This sphere in particular can least of all be cleanly separated from its Graeco-Roman environment. There is already a series of admirable or at least stimulating works on the question of 'Hellenistic influence', though this particular area of research is still far from being exhausted. Here I can call attention to the investigations of R.Meyer,[270] S.Lieberman[271] and also the *Essays in Graeco-Roman and Related Talmudic Literature*, edited by H.A.Fischel.[272] One thing that we particularly need is a new collection of Greek and Latin loanwords; the indispensable work by S.Krauss[273] needs a thorough linguistic and methodological revision.

Josephus compared the Pharisees with the Stoics, and some amazing parallels can be established here, though they relate more to a certain basic ethical and religious attitude than to demonstrable direct influences. In what follows I shall merely pick out some well known examples which make it clear that the Pharisaic sages, too, paid their tribute to the spirit of the age and participated in the religious *koine* of their time.

David Daube[274] and Günther Mayer[275] have given a remarkable demonstration of the way in which the rabbinic interpretation of scripture, allegedly grounded on Hillel's seven hermeneutical rules, ultimately has its model in the methods of Alexandrian philologists and jurists. The closest parallel to the Pharisaic chain of tradition lies in the succession of heads in Greek philosophical schools; the Jewish Passover Seder is a collection of paradigms for Greek customs at table which already play a role in Ben Sira. Here the festal custom of the leading class who recline on comfortable couches discussing and singing in their symposia is transferred to the religious festal celebration of the whole people. Discussions with pagan 'philosophers' and knowledge of some of their views can be instanced in the Talmud as frequently as can elements from Greek mythology. Thus the rabbinic doctrine of souls, including the doctrine of the pre-existence of the soul, is largely dependent on ideas from popular philosophy. The rabbis knew the *sifre homeros*,[276] the books of Homer, and saw them as an *adiaphoron* which did not make the hands unclean, as did the holy scriptures.

The four elements of the Greeks were used to illustrate the creation story, and even the myth of the androgynous primal man was taken over. *'Androginōs* becomes a loanword in the Talmud. An image of the transmigration of souls, the wheel of time which constantly turns, is also taken over.[277] The legend of Alexander is highly esteemed and there is knowledge of the myth of the death of Osiris and the image of the suckling Isis, the sagas of the Danaids' cask, Ariadne's thread, Procrustes' bed, the myth of the phoenix, the Sirens (already in the Septuagint) and the Centaurs. Animal fables in the style of Aesop and Hellenistic dream-stories were also popular. S.Lieberman brought out numerous Greek sentences, pieces of gnomic wisdom and word-plays in the rabbinic literature.[278]

In conclusion I would like to go on to refer to some well-known traditions about Hillel.[279] Here mention should first be made of the prosbol (προσβολή) regulation which did away with the detrimental social side-effects of the commandments relating to the seventh year when debts were cancelled (Deut. 15); the summary of the whole of the Torah in the golden rule;[280] and the definition of the soul as a 'guest in the body' – though this is set alongside the requirement to cherish the body as the divine image of God.[281] The command to love all men, the stress on study, an almost Cynic asceticism and a striving for autarky, and the concern to win pagans over to the truth of the Torah of God are also in line with this.[282] Perhaps we could see this attitude – which became legendary – as an authentic alternative to the development of Hellenistic splendour in Herodian Jerusalem. In its turn it was indebted not just to the spirit of the Old Testament but also (whether consciously or not) to the Socratic humanitarian tradition.[283] Not only Christianity but also rabbinic Judaism, which is different in so many other ways, basically rests on a synthesis.

6

The Consequences: Palestinian Judaism as 'Hellenistic' Judaism

This brief and very fragmentary sketch of the 'Hellenizing' of Jewish Palestine has many consequences for our understanding of the history of earliest Christianity. I would like to bring out just four points:

1. Since after a more than three-hundred-year history under the influence of Greek culture Palestinian Judaism can also be described as 'Hellenistic Judaism', *the term 'Hellenistic' as currently used no longer serves to make any meaningful differentiation in terms of the history of religions within the history of earliest Christianity.* A sentence like that written by F.Büchsel, 'The underlying basis of his view of life is that of Palestinian Judaism and not Alexandrian Judaism contaminated with Hellenism',[284] is no longer defensible in that form. If anywhere, it will have been in Palestine that Judaism will have been 'contaminated with Hellenism', but this predicate is intrinsically quite absurd and in this connection must be ruled out from the start. We must stop attaching either negative or positive connotations to the question of 'Hellenistic' influence. It may again have become popular to play off the (Old Testament) Jewish spirit against the Greek (and vice versa), but such evaluations do not get us any further. Judaism and Christianity, indeed our whole Western world, have become what they are as a result of both the Old Testament *and* the Greek tradition. First of all we must be concerned with the historical connections, which are more complicated and more complex than our labels, clichés and pigeon-holes, but at the same time also with a real understanding and an evaluation which does justice to the past and is no longer one-sided and tendentious.

2. We should therefore be more cautious in using the adjective 'Hellenistic' in descriptions of earliest Christianity. *It says too much, and precisely because of that says too little.* In this matter of establishing

the history of a small Jewish messianic sect with its roots in Palestine, which is so difficult, we need more precise differentiations for our reconstruction and understanding of the first hundred years. First of all there is the difference in language between Greek and Aramaic, which already begins in Galilee and Jerusalem; then there is the difference in level of language brought about by education, between the simple *koine* and rhetorically polished Greek; then there are the sociological differences, between city and country, between slaves, day labourers, tax farmers, the middle class and the aristocracy. Further possible distinctions arise as a result of differences in geographical regions and cities – between Galilee and Judaea, Jerusalem and Antioch, Asia Minor and Rome, and finally, last but not least, as a result of personal relationships to authorities, bearers of traditions and schools: Paul, Peter, John, James, etc. Anyone who uses the word 'Hellenistic' should define it more precisely. It has too many aspects. Does it simply mean 'Greek in the late period' or 'oriental syncretistic'? Does it refer to technology, art, economics, politics, rhetoric and literature, philosophy or religion? Might it even simply mean 'pagan', as it did later, from the third century on? It is this multiplicity which makes our theme so difficult, especially as a great variety of nuances has come together. Or does it relate to ancient Greek myth, to Iranian, Egyptian, Babylonian or even Gnostic mythology? (This last usage is particularly popular and misleading.)[285] Unqualified use of the term Hellenistic no longer produces clarity; it simply increases the historical confusion which as it is threatens our discipline.

3. Moreover, we must reckon with the possibility that much more intellectual development was *possible* in Jewish Palestine than scholarship is prepared to accept. What was *impossible* can be listed quickly: a blatantly pagan cult, i.e. a clear break with the first commandment (and the second), an obvious and lasting failure to observe essential parts of the Torah, and specific desecration of the temple. Here, however, one may not presuppose the casuistically refined Pharisaic understanding of the Torah, since we do not know how far this had become completely established among the people – for example in Galilee – as early as the time of Jesus. Certainly the Pharisees had the greatest influence on the people, but they did not yet have absolute spiritual mastery over them. It even remains questionable whether, when and to what extent the rabbis achieved this later. This impossibility of openly criticizing the Torah and the temple already proved to be the downfall of the Hellenists, as it later proved to be that of Paul. For this reason I also regard a pre-Pauline

mission among Gentiles in Palestine, the heartland of Judaism, which took no account of the law, as having been quite impossible. In peripheral areas like the coastal plain, the cities of the Decapolis or the Phoenician coast the situation may already have been quite dfferent.

On the other hand, the whole development of christological doctrine *could* have taken place completely within Palestinian Judaism. There it was possible to find several pre-existent heavenly mediators closely bound up with God. Even the title ὁ κύριος must already have been transferred to Jesus in Jerusalem. Nevertheless, James and the other brothers of Jesus allowed themselves to be called 'the Lord's brothers' (ἀδελφοὶ τοῦ κυρίου), and later they and subsequent kinsfolk of the Lord were given the similar designation δεσπόσυνοι.[286] There is hardly any doctrinal theme in the New Testament which could not also have been thought or taught in Palestine. The problems which led to the persecution of the Christians there did not consist primarily in 'dogmatic' questions, but in questions relating to the specific observance of the Torah. Even a christology of pre-existence and of the Son of God is intrinsically not 'Hellenistic' nor even 'un-Jewish' nor 'un-Palestinian'. To take one instance, there are other reasons why we do not conjecture that the hymn in Philippians came into being in the Jerusalem community – they are historical and philological ones. The hymn seems to me to be typically Pauline. Generally speaking, however, we must be more cautious in our hypotheses about the kergyma of the earliest Christian community in Jerusalem, or better, more generous. Between 30 and 50 CE in Jerusalem there was more creativity and there were more intellectual possibilities 'than are dreamed of in our philosophy'. By contrast, we must assume that there was a degree of regression in the late community under James from the end of the 40s under the pressure of changed political circumstances.

4. One last point has to do with the problem of the sociology of education. With the possible exceptions of Luke and the author of Hebrews, the New Testament authors, who were overwhelmingly Jewish Christians, had no deeper acquaintance with secular Greek writing. They either completely lacked real Greek education, obtained through well-known 'classical literature', as in the case of Mark, Matthew or John (and probably also Paul), or their knowledge was very fragmentary. As a rule the New Testament authors came from the synagogue training of the Greek-speaking Jewish community of Palestine and the Diaspora, where of course there were considerable

qualitative differences between individual synagogues. It is precisely over this point of the lack of a deeper literary Greek education within the predominant canon of literature which began with Homer and included the tragedians up to Euripides[287] that earliest Christianity and the mass of Palestinian (and 'Hellenistic') Judaism had something fundamentally in common. Despite any knowledge of the Greek language, access to higher education was confined to a very thin upper stratum. We can see from Petronius's *Cena Trimalchionis* that not every *nouveau riche* who counted himself a member of the upper class was really educated. The usual Jewish-'Hellenistic' education in the mother country and in Palestine had another basis. People probably read the Septuagint and other edifying and entertaining 'Jewish-Greek' literature, but very rarely the Greek classic writers and philosophers in the original. Moreover, it was not literature which had the greatest missionary effect in the first and second centuries, but Jewish and Christian preaching, oral discussions and personal testimony in word and action, encounters which led to participation in the synagogue services or meetings of the Christian community. We may assume that those men who bore the new message from Jewish Palestine to Syria and Asia Minor and indeed to Rome came neither from the illiterate proletariat nor from the aristocracy but from the creative middle class, which nowadays is so readily dismissed as 'petty-bourgeois', a social milieu from which Jesus and Paul probably came.

This situation lasted basically throughout the first century, and clearly changed only during the course of the second century. The first harbingers of a more solid literary Greek education are Luke, the author of Hebrews, and Clement of Rome.[288] The real change came relatively late, about the time of the emperor Hadrian (117-38), with the first significant Gnostics, Basilides and Valentinus, with Marcion, and around the same time with the Apologists.[289] The overcoming of this educational limitation was far more decisive than the move from Palestinian to 'Hellenistic' Jewish Christianity which is so problematical.[290]

Only then do we have the beginning of what, in Harnack's words, was the final 'Hellenizing of Christianity'.[291]

Notes

1. This sketch was presented for the first time *in nuce* to a group of New Testament scholars at the Annual Conference for Academic Theology in Göttingen in 1976, and in 1982 it formed the basis of a seminar in Bern in preparation for a visit to Israel. In the meantime it has been worked over and expanded a number of times. Abbreviated versions were given as lectures in autumn 1988 in King's College, London, and Wolfson College, Oxford, and in a slightly different form it was the basis for a lecture in the Wissenschaftskolleg in Berlin, in the Free University of Berlin and the Leipzig Theological Seminar. I am grateful to Christoph Markschies for his collaboration in the collection and formulation of the notes and for the writing of the various growing versions. Our conversation together has accompanied the maturing of this short work over the past year.

2. Here possibly there is still indirect influence from F.C.Baur. In the first volume of his *The Church History of the First Three Centuries* (^{3}1863, ET London 1878-9) he presents Christianity as 'absolute religion' and thus as a synthesis of Jewish and Greek preliminary forms in the process of disintegration (p.6). However, Christianity has a 'far closer and more direct relationship to Judaism' (ibid.); the same view is also expressed in Baur's *Paul the Apostle of Jesus Christ, His Life and Work, His Epistles and His Doctrine. A Contribution to a Critical History of Primitive Christianity* (^{2}1867), London ^{2}1875, 250-2.

For an assessment of Judaism in German scholarship see now C.Hoffmann, *Juden und Judentum im Werk Deutscher Althistoriker des 19. und 20. Jahrhunderts*, Studies in Judaism in Modern Times 9, Leiden 1988.

3. On this see some recent investigations by F.Millar, especially for the pre-Roman period, which is 'Hellenistic' in the authentic sense, in which sources for the heartland of Syria are relatively sparse: 'The Problem of Hellenistic Syria', in *Hellenism in the East. The Interaction of Greek and Non-Greek Civilizations from Syria to Central Asia after Alexander*, ed. A.Kuhrt and S.Sherwin-White, London 1987, 110-84, with an extensive bibliography; for the Roman period see id., 'Empire, Community and Culture in the Roman Near East: Greeks, Syrians, Jews and Arabs', *JJS* 38, 1987, 143-64; for the special case of the Phoenicians, with whom the 'process of fusion' with Greek culture already begins in the Persian period, develops continuously and is completed in the period of the Principate, see id., 'The Phoenician Cities: A Case-Study

of Hellenization', *PCPS* 209, 1983, 55-71; finally in addition the numerous contributions in *ANRW* II.8, *Politische Geschichte (Provinzen und Randvölker: Syrien, Palästina, Arabien)*, ed. H.Temporini and W.Haase, Berlin and New York 1977.

4. In his Tübingen inaugural lecture (*Urchristentum, Spätjudentum, Hellenismus, Akademische Antrittsvorlesung, gehalten am 28 Oktober 1926*, Stuttgart 1926), G.Kittel argued against making the dividing line between the two cultural worlds 'simply in a crude and mechanical way' (10), referring to K.Holl's Rectoral Address 'Urchristentum und Religionsgeschichte' (it appeared first in *ZSTh* 2, 1924, 387-430, later in id., *Gesammelte Aufsätze zur Kirchengeschichte*, 2. *Der Osten*, Tübingen 1928 [reissued Darmstadt 1964], 1-32; cf. G.Kittel, *Die Probleme des palästinischen Spätjudentums und das Urchristentum*, BWANT 3,1, Stuttgart 1926, 72: 'People are largely inclined to underestimate the problem of Palestinian Judaism in the history of religions or to regard it as simpler than it is.' Although Kittel resolutely refused to see the Judaism of Palestine as a syncretistic phenomenon, he stressed that 'the whirlpool of political and spiritual movements of those centuries did not pass it by', and that there were 'circles which deliberately yielded to the alien "modern" influences'; furthermore there were 'without doubt the manifold imperceptible influences to which official and even more unofficial popular Judaism could hardly keep itself completely closed, whether it wanted to or not' (74). Nevertheless the same author stresses in *Die Religionsgeschichte und das Urchristentum*, Gütersloh 1931 (reissued Darmstadt 1959), 11: 'So the coming into being of Christianity, too, cannot be understood in any other way: the first Christians were subjects of the Roman empire, either Palestinian Jews *or* (my italics) members of the circle of Hellenistic culture.' Would it not have been more realistic to say that to different degrees they were both? On this see the impressive remarks on 42-106.

In the third edition of W.Bousset's *Die Religion des Judentums im späthellenistischen Zeitalter*, edited by H.Gressmann, HNT 21, Tübingen [4]1966, the different forms of religion in the Hellenistic period have also influenced late-Hellenistic Judaism, described (quite wrongly) as 'imitative and uncreative' (472), although the 'opposition to the Hellenistic spirit' remains more significant than all the influences (484). For protest against this interpretation of Judaism as a 'syncretistic religion' see Kittel, *Probleme*, 11f., 75 n.4, and id., *Religionsgeschichte*, 66ff. The whole discussion shows how complicated the problem is and also the relative vagueness of the terms 'Hellenism' or 'syncretism' which are so popular for use almost as watchwords. It is correct that apart from the episode after 168/7 BCE which led to the Maccabaean revolt, real Jewish-pagan forms of *religion* are virtually absent from Jewish Palestine and can be found very rarely in the Diaspora, but this still does not amount to an independence from the dominant Hellenistic civilization, its modes of life and thought, which also extended their influence into the religious sphere.

The opposition between 'Judaism' and 'Hellenism' is also mentioned by L.Goppelt, *Christentum und Judentum im ersten und zweiten Jahrhundert. Ein Aufriss der Urgeschichte der Kirche*, BFCT 2.R. 55, Gütersloh 1954, 21; according to P.Wendland, earliest Christianity was originally 'an alien body over against Hellenism' ('Die griechische Prosa', in *Einleitung in die Altertumswissenschaft*, ed. A.Gercke and E.Norden, I. *Methodik, Sprache, Metrik, Griechische und Römische Literatur*, Leipzig and Berlin 1910, 329-98: 385). Here, however, Wendland uses an earlier concept of 'Hellenism' which identifies Hellenism with higher Greek education (see below on Harnack, n.291) and not the concept of Hellenism current in the History of Religions school which was stamped by the idea of an 'oriental syncretism'. Amazingly, W.Bousset agreed with this insight repeated by Wendland in his contribution to Lietzmann's HNT (*Die hellenistisch-römische Welt in ihren Beziehungen zu Judentum und Christentum*, HNT 1/2, Tübingen 1907) in his review of the book ('Ein grundlegender Beitrag zur Religionsgeschichte des neutestamentlichen Zeitalters', *ThR* 11, 1908, 323-41:336). But because he regarded 'late Judaism' as being pure Pharisaism (W.Bousset, *Jesu Predigt in ihrem Gegensatz zum Judentum. Ein religionsgeschichtlicher Vergleich*, Göttingen 1892, 32), on the other hand he wrote: 'But Jesus is... heavens removed from the nature of Jewish thinking' (46). Just as R.Bultmann's much-read account, *Primitive Christianity in its Contemporary Setting*, London and New York 1956, has a division between its discussion of Judaism (59-102) and that of Hellenism (135-74), so too the widely-circulated introduction by E.Lohse (*The New Testament Environment*, Nashville and London 1976) has as its two main parts 'Judaism in the Time of the New Testament' (15-196) and 'The Hellenistic-Roman Environment of the New Testament' (197-277).

5. Thus for example the sub-division of the paragraphs in *TDNT*; on this see articles by G.Friedrich, ' "Begriffsgeschichtliche" Untersuchungen zum Theologischen Wörterbuch zum Neuen Testament', *ABG* 22, 1976, 151-77; id., 'Die Problematik eines Theologisches Wörterbuch zum Neuen Testament', in *Studia Evangelica*, TU 73, Berlin 1959, 481-6, with id., 'Das bisher noch fehlende Begriffslexikon zum Neuen Testament', *NTS* 19, 1972/73, 127-52.

6. Here are a few random examples: K.Holl's questioning (in 'Urchristentum und Religionsgeschichte' [n.4], 5-7) of Reitzenstein's derivations from the 'mystery religions' or E.Norden's protest against the characterization of Christianity as 'syncretistic religion' (in *Die Geburt des Kindes. Geschichte einer religiösen Idee* [1924], Darmstadt ³1958, 111): he says that the formula is 'dangerous as it raises what is secondary to the rank of an essential, and leaves out of account the real decisive factor which made the new religion burst out of the ring of all... the earlier dominant religions'. H.Gunkel (*Zum religionsgeschichtlichen Verständnis des Neuen Testaments*, FRLANT 1, Göttingen 1903, 88, 95), for example, had spoken of 'syncretistic' religion. A more recent specific problem similarly illustrates what I have just said. According to K.Wengst, *Christologische Formeln und Lieder des Urchristentums*, StNT 7, Gütersloh 1972, Judaism took over the idea of an atoning death from the Greeks: 'This idea of "dying for" has a long tradition in the Greek world' (67); Wengst therefore rejects any derivation from the Aramaic-speaking

primitive community or from Palestinian Judaism. Against this see my *The Atonement. A Study of the Origins of the Doctrine in the New Testament*, London 1981, 19, 64, 76-93; and *The Son of God. The Origin of Christology and the History of Jewish-Hellenistic Religion*, London and Philadelphia 1976 (there is a second revised and enlarged German edition, *Der Sohn Gottes*, Tübingen 1977, see 32-4, 35-89; in English both are now included in *The Cross of the Son of God*, London 1986, 207, 252, 264-281), and K.T.Kleinknecht, *Der leidende Gerechtfertigte. Die alttestamentlich-jüdische Tradition vom 'leidenden Gerechten' und ihre Rezeption bei Paulus*, WUNT 2.R. 13, Tübingen 1985, 51, 66, 177.

Another example (among many) is the dispute over the conception of the 'body of Christ': see E.Käsemann, *Leib und Leib Christi. Eine Untersuchung zur paulinischen Begrifflichkeit*, BHT 9, Tübingen 1933; H.Schlier, *Christus und Kirche im Epheserbrief*, BHT 6, Tübingen 1930, and the two articles by E.Schweizer, 'Die Kirche als Leib Christi in den paulinischen Homologoumena bzw. Antilegomena', first in *TLZ* 86, 1961, 161-74, 241-56, in id., *Neotestamentica. Deutsche Aufsätze 1951-1963*, Zurich and Stuttgart 1963, 272-92 and 293-316; finally H.Merklein, 'Enstehung und Gehalt des paulinischen Leib-Christi-Gedankens', in id., *Studien zu Jesus und Paulus*, WUNT 43, Tübingen 1987, 319-44.

Only very recently, in a comprehensive review, the absurd objection has been made against what in my view is the urgent task of a 'biblical theology' that 'The intertestamental period (in part) and the Hellenistic world cannot be thrust into the background in this way as being of lesser importance' (O.Merk, 'Gesamtbiblische Theologie. Zum Fortgang der Diskussion in den 80er Jahren', *VF* 33, 1988, 19-40:38). As though Daniel, Koheleth, Esther or Proverbs 1-10 did not belong in the Hellenistic period, quite apart from Tobit, Judith, Sirach, I and II Maccabees and Wisdom, which are parts of the traditional *Christian* Bible: strictly speaking there was no 'intertestamental' period. This term which is often used is neither Jewish (because for Jews there is only one 'testament') nor really Christian (the Old Testament ends with John the Baptist, Luke 16.16). It is possibly Calvinistic orthodoxy, where the 'Old Testament' ends with the Hebrew canon in the time of 'Malachi' (which never was) or Ezra. Anyone who thinks that adjectives like 'scientific' or 'historical-critical' can be carried around like a monstrance ought by now to take notice of clear *historical facts*.

We can study the dispute paradigmatically by the different attempts at derivation of the Johannine prologue: the 'Tübingen school' once associated it with the philosophical Logos speculation of Alexandria; the History of Religions school derived it from 'Gnostic syncretism'; H.Gese ('The Prologue to John's Gospel', in id., *Essays on Biblical Theology*, Minneapolis 1981, 167-222) differs radically in looking at it in terms of the history of the Old Testament wisdom tradition. For the history of its exegesis in the nineteenth and twentieth centuries, see now M.Theobald, *Die Fleischwerdung des Logos*, NTA.NF 20, Münster 1988, though he fails to do justice to the complicated problems connected with the history of religions (55-67 on Bultmann).

7. A typical example – among countless others – is the section 'Hellenisti-

scher Enthusiasmus' in the article 'Eschatologie IV (im NT)' by G.Klein (*TRE* 10, Berlin and New York 1982, 278-99). According to W.Schmithals ('Eschatologie und Apokalyptik', *VF* 33, 1988, 68), even before Paul the powerful heresy of Christian Gnosticism arises out of a pre-Christian Gnostic-dualistic enthusiasm, which is said to be as old as the Jewish apocalyptic related to it (thus W.Schmithals, *The Apocalyptic Movement. Introduction and Interpretation*, Nashville 1975, 69 – one can hardly deal more violently with historical reality!). But do we not have to describe the Essene self-awareness which celebrates the liturgy of the community in communion with the angels and the innermost sanctity of God, or the religious claim to power of the *yōrdē merkaba*, even more as 'enthusiastic Hellenistic Judaism'? D.Georgi ('Weisheit Salomos', JSHRZ 3.4, *Unterweisungen in lehrhafter Form*, Gütersloh 1980, 394) similarly sees the Wisdom of Solomon as a 'Gnostic writing', indeed 'the oldest that we possess'. Here one is really tempted to talking of contraventions of the Trade Descriptions Act!

8. W.Heitmüller, 'Zum Problem Paulus und Jesus', first in *ZNW* 13, 1912, 320-37, in *Das Paulusbild in der neueren deutschen Forschung*, ed. K.H.Rengstorf in collaboration with U.Luck, WdF 24, Darmstadt 1969, 124-43, esp. 134f., 138-42. In addition to older accounts (Goppelt, *Christentum und Judentum* [n.4]; F.Hahn, *Christologische Hoheitstitel. Ihre Geschichte im frühen Christentum*, FRLANT 83, Göttingen ³1966; id., *Mission in the New Testament*, SBT 47, London 1965), see now C.Colpe, 'Die älteste judenchristliche Gemeinde', in *Die Anfänge des Christentums. Alte Welt und neue Hoffnung*, Stuttgart, Berlin, Cologne and Mainz 1987, 59-79; K.M.Fischer, *Das Urchristentum*, Kirchenge-schichte in Einzeldarstellungen I/1, Berlin 1985, 78-86 ('Das hellenistische Urchristentum'). There is a detailed discussion of the theme in my 'Christol-ogy and New Testament Chronology: A Problem in the History of Earliest Christianity' and 'Between Jesus and Paul. The "Hellenists", the "Seven" and Stephen (Acts 6.1-15; 7.54-8.3)', in *Between Jesus and Paul*, London and Philadelphia 1983, 30-47 and 156-66, 1-29 and 129-56 respectively.

9. Cf. C.Andresen, *Geschichte des Christentums* I. *Von den Anfängen bis zur Hochscholastik*, TW 6, Stuttgart, Berlin, Cologne and Mainz 1975, or H.Lietz-mann, *History of the Early Church* 1, *The Beginnings*, London 1937, with W.Schneemelcher, *Das Urchristentum*, UB 336, Stuttgart, Berlin, Cologne and Mainz 1981, 100ff., 123ff., 155ff., though he presents what in my view is a questionable picture of earliest Christianity which in terms of the present state of scholarship is obsolete, because he completely underestimates the creative power and variety of ancient Judaism in the mother country and in the Diaspora.

10. R.Bultmann, 'Die Bedeutung der neuerschlossenen mandäischen und manichäischen Quellen für das Verständnis des Johannesevangeliums', first published in *ZNW* 24, 1925, 100-46, and in id., *Exegetica. Aufsätze zur Erforschung des Neuen Testaments*, selected and edited with an introduction by E.Dinkler, Tübingen 1967, 102f.

11. W.Fauth, 'Dea Syria', *KP* 1, Munich 1979, 1400-3; M.Hörig, 'Dea Syria – Atargatis', *ANRW* II, 17.3, Berlin and New York 1984, 1536-81.

12. For this see F.Millar (above n.3); on Antioch see G.Downey, *A History of Antioch in Syria*, Princeton 1961; id., *Ancient Antioch*, Princeton 1963; for the Roman period, see J.Lassus, 'La ville d'Antioche à l'époque romain d'après l'archéologie', *ANRW* II.8 (n.3), 54-102. So monumental a work as P.M.Frazer, *Ptolemaic Alexandria* (three vols), Oxford 1972, could not be written about Hellenistic and early Roman Antioch. The really great period of the city, in which there are abundant sources, lies in the fourth century, in the time of Libanius and the great Antiochene church fathers, see J.H.W.G.Liebeschuetz, *Antioch, City and Imperial Administration in the Later Roman Empire*, Oxford 1972. For Damascus see K.Tümpel, 'Damaskos', *PW* IV.2, Stuttgart 1901, 2042-8: 2045f. The first reports of the internal constitution of the city as a Hellenistic *polis* come from the account of his family by Nicolaus of Damascus, see Millar, 'The Problem of Hellenistic Syria' (n.3), 125f. and below pp.35f.

13. F.Bolgiani, 'Diatesseron', *Dizionario Patristico e di Antichità Cristiane* I, Casale Monferrato 1983, 945-7.

14. See Millar, 'Empire, Community and Culture' (n.3), 152, 159f. These three texts – the 'Edessene Chronicle', the letter of Mara Bar Sarapion and the 'Book of the Laws of the Lands' of Bardesanes (quite apart from the other Christian-Gnostic works) – are basically already influenced by Christianity. For the whole question see also A.Baumstark, *Geschichte der Syrischen Literatur*, Bonn 1922, 10-14, and H.J.W.Drijvers, 'Hatra, Palmyra und Edessa. Die Städte der syrisch-mesopotamischen Wüste in politischer, kulturgeschichtlicher und religionsgeschichtlicher Beleuchtung', *ANRW* II.8 (n.4), 799-906, and id., *Cults and Beliefs at Edessa*, EPRO 82, Leiden 1982.

15. M.Hörig, 'Dea Syria' (n.11), 1537f. It should be noted that both the cult of Emesa and the caravan city of Palmyra have less an 'Aramaic' than an 'Arabian' background, see Millar, 'Empire, Community and Culture' (n.3), 155-9; Drijvers, 'Hatra, Palmyra and Edessa', *ANRW* II.8 (n.4), 837f.; R.D.Sullivan, 'The Dynasty of Emesa', ibid., 198-219. Julia Domna, the daughter of Julius Bassianus, the priest of Sol Elagabalus, married Septimius Severus, who himself came from an originally Punic family in Leptis Magna in Tripolitania. Her great nephew Elagabalus became emperor in 218 (cf. id., 'Priesthoods of the Eastern Dynastic Aristocracy', in *Studien zur Religion und Kultur Kleinasiens. FS K.Dörner zum 65.Geburtstag*, ed. S.Sahin, E.Schwertheim and J.Wagner, EPRO 66, Vol.2, Leiden 1978, 914-39. Only in the third century was Juvenal's well-known complaint fully realized: '*Iam pridem Syrus in Tiberim defluxit Orontes*' (*Satires*, 3.62).

16. See my *Judaism and Hellenism. Studies in their Encounter in Palestine in the Early Hellenistic Period*, London and Philadelphia 1974, I, 296-301.

17. H.Gese, 'Die Religionen Altsyriens', in *Die Religionen Altsyriens, Altarabiens und der Mandäer*, RM 10/2, Stuttgart, Berlin, Cologne and Mainz 1970, 216-29; J.Teixidor, *The Pagan God. Popular Religion in the Greco-Roman Near East*, Princeton 1977, esp.5ff.,11f.; id., *The Pantheon of Palmyra*, EPRO 79, Leiden 1979; there is also further literature in id., 'Religion und Kult in Palmyra', in *Palmyra. Geschichte, Kunst und Kultur der syrischen Oasenstadt. Einführende Beiträge*

und Katalog zur Ausstellung, Linz 1987, 32-43:41f.; G.H.Halsberghe, *The Cult of Sol Invictus*, EPRO 23, Leiden 1972; id., 'Le culte de Deus Sol Invictus à Rome au 3ᵉ siècle après J.C.', *ANRW* II.17/4, Berlin and New York 1984, 2181-201.

18. Bultmann's conjectures on the influence of Gnostic 'mystery communities' in which the redeemer was identified with the Phrygian mystery god Attis, as a result of which the Gnostic movement will also have penetrated the Christian communities, are utterly fantastic (*The Theology of the New Testament*, 1, London and New York 1952, 171). Such a combination (viz. of Attis and a Gnostic redeemer) is said even to have preceded Paul (ibid., 298; cf. id., *Primitive Christianity* [n.1], 162 – in both cases without any evidence!). Bultmann probably derives this hypothesis on the one hand from the *very* much later report by Hippolytus on the Naassenes (*Haer.* 5.6.3-5.11, ed. P.Wendland, GCS, 77-104, and there in particular the hymns to Attis, 9.8f., ed. Wendland, 99f.); cf. also L.Abramowski, 'Ein gnostischer Logostheologe. Umfang und Redaktor des gnostischen Sonderguts in Hippolyts "Widerlegung aller Häresien"', in id., *Drei christologische Untersuchungen*, BZNW 45, Berlin and New York 1981, 18-62: 46-56, and J.Frickel, *Hellenistische Erlösung in christlicher Deutung. Die gnostische Naassenerschrift. Quellenkritische Studien – Strukturanalyse – Schichtenscheidung – Rekonstruktion der Anthropos-Lehrschrift*, NHS 19, Leiden 1984, and from works by R.Reitzenstein (*Die hellenistischen Mysterienreligionen. Ihre Grundgedanken und Mitwirkungen*, Berlin and Leipzig ³1927, reissued Darmstadt 1956, 12ff., 108, 145, 152, 181, 241, etc.: as far as its dating of the texts and location of them in the history of religions is concerned, this work can without qualification be said to be completely fantastic). Reizenstein had extracted a Gnostic source, the Naassene sermon, from Hippolytus's account and 'twice reprinted the basic text derived in this way' (Abramowski, 'Logostheologe', 46, with reference to Reitzenstein, *Poimandres. Studien zur griechisch-ägyptischen und frühchristlichen Literatur*, Leipzig 1904, 83-98, and Reitzenstein and H.H.Schaeder, *Studien zum antiken Synkretismus aus Iran und Griechenland*, SBW 7, Leipzig and Berlin 1926, reissued Darmstadt 1965, 161-73).

19. For this see my *Judaism and Hellenism* (n.16), 1f.; also 'Between Jesus and Paul'(n.8), 9 and 141f.n.63 (with examples). R.Bichler, *'Hellenismus'. Geschichte und Problematik eines Epochenbegriffes*, Impulse der Forschung 41, Darmstadt 1983 is informative but generally questionable.

20. Cf. *A Patristic Greek Lexicon*, ed. G.W.H.Lampe, Oxford ⁸1987, 451. The title of Tatian's 'accusation' (λόγος πρὸς Ἕλληνας) shows a first tendency in this direction; around 170 the apologist Apollinaris of Laodicea is said to have composed five books 'To the Hellenes' which have been lost (Eusebius, HE 4.27.1). However, here the word still means 'educated *Greek*' and not 'non-Christian' generally.

21. Hengel, 'Between Jesus and Paul' (n.8), 6; but cf. already W.Jaeger, *Early Christianity and Greek Paideia*, Cambridge, Mass. and London 1962, 5f.

22. Only later was the meaning 'Gentile' introduced here. This false interpretation resulted in the misleading reading Ἑλληνιστάς in Acts 11.20 (thus Vaticanus, the corrected Codex Bezae, the Basiliensis and Athous

Laurensis with the majority text of the continuous witnesses and Nestle-Aland[26]) instead of Ἕλληνας (thus still Nestle-Aland[25] with p[74], the corrected Sinaiticus, Alexandrinus and the original text of Codex Bezae).

23. 'Knowledge of Greek in aristocratic and military circles of Judaism can already be demonstrated on the basis of the Zeno papyri between 260 and 250 BCE in Palestine' (*Judaism and Hellenism*, I, 8–11, 60f., 103f., 286f., see also my *Jews, Greeks and Barbarians*, London and Philadelphia 1980, 57 ; cf. J.A.Fitzmyer, 'The Languages of Palestine in the First Century AD', *CBQ* 32, 1970, 501-31). Fitzmyer mentions as the earliest text in Palestine an inscription of a priest of Ptolemy IV Philopator (222-205) from Jaffa from 217 BCE (508); a fragment of an inscription from the Idumaean capital Marisa also comes from the same period, after the victory of Philopator at Raphia in 217, see also *SEG* 7, 1937, 326 (and Polybius 5.61.9): the victorious king had himself celebrated in the province with inscriptions; cf. B.Lifshitz, 'Beiträge zur palästinischen Epigraphik', *ZDPV* 78, 1962, 82-4, and Millar, 'Problem of Hellenistic Syria' (n.3), 114f., 118, 132f. Mention should also be made of the designations of three musical instruments in Dan.3.5 deriving from Greek words (on this see Fitzmyer, 'Languages', 509, and *Judaism and Hellenism* II, 43 n.18) and the dedicatory inscription of a Greek(-Macedonian) family to him and Serapis in Samaria, *SEG* 8, 1937, 93 (*Judaism and Hellenism* II, 102 n.337). Some ostraca are even later, like one from Jerusalem with two Greek loanwords (F.M.Cross, 'An Aramaic Ostracon of the Third Century BCE from Excavations in Jerusalem', *ErIs* 15, 1981, 67*-9*) and another from Elath on the Gulf of Akaba (N.Glueck, 'Ostraca from Elath', *BASOR* 80, 1940, 3-10: 8f.). We should add to this a bilingual ostracon from Khirbet el Qôm from the late third or early second century, first reported by J.S.Holladay in 'Notes and News', *IEJ* 21, 1971, 175-7: 176; cf. L.Geraty, 'The Khirbet el-Kôm Bilingual Ostracon', *BASOR* 220, 1975, 55-61, with A.Skaist, 'A Note on the Bilingual Ostracon from Khirbet el-Kôm', *IEJ* 28, 1978, 106-8, and Millar, 'Problem of Hellenistic Syria', 118, and the bilingual inscription from Dan, Θεῷ [τ]ῷ ἐν Δανοῖς [Ζ]ωίλος εὐχήν with the line in small Aramaic characters under this text: *ndr zyls l'* (text e.g. in *SEG* 31, 1981, 1455, see A.Biran and V.Tzaferis, 'A Bilingual Dedicatory Inscription from Tel Dan', *Qad.* 10, 1977, 114f.; or A.Biran, in *Temples and High Places in Biblical Times*, Jerusalem 1981, 145-7 with Plate 20.4). According to Millar ('Problem', 132) this is the only bilingual Aramaic-Greek inscription and the only Aramaic inscription from Syrian territory in the Hellenistic/pre-Roman period. We also have a few early Greek traces, perhaps from as early as the third century BCE, from Shechem in Samaria, see *Judaism and Hellenism* I, 62. Numerous Greek inscriptions occur in the second century, see Millar, 'Phoenician Cities' (n.3), 63. The great inscription from Hefzibah near Scythopolis comes from the period after 200, see Y.H.Landau, 'A Greek Inscription found near Hefzibah', *IEJ* 16, 1966, 56-70; T.Fischer, 'Zur Seleukideninschrift von Hefzibah', *ZPE* 33, 1979, 31-8; J.M.Bertrand, 'Sur l'inscription d'Hefzibah', *ZPE* 46, 1982, 167-76.

24. P.Rüger, 'Zum Problem der Sprache Jesu', *ZNW* 59, 1968, 113-22; R.Degen, 'Aramäisch I', and P.Rüger, 'Aramäisch II', *TRE* 3, 1978, 599-610.

25. Y.Meshorer, *Jewish Coins of the Second Temple Period*, Tel Aviv 1967, Plates II/III, nos.5, 5a, 7, 8, 9: ΒΑΣΙΛΕΩΣ ΑΛΕΞΑΝΔΡΟΥ, cf. Schürer, *History* I, 219-28, 603f. (E.Schürer, *The History of the Jewish People in the Age of Jesus Christ (175 BC- AD 135)*, A New English Version, Vol.I and II rev. and ed. by G.Vermes, F.Millar and M.Black, Edinburgh 1973, 1979; Vol.III/1,2 rev. and ed. by G.Vermes, F.Millar and M.Goodman, Edinburgh 1986, 1987).

26. Schürer, *History* I (n.25), 578, 582, and Y.Meshorer, 'Nabataean Coins', *Qedem* 3, Jerusalem 1975, 86f.

27. Y.Meshorer, *Jewish Coins* (n.25), 64; also Plates VI-XVIII with legend, 127-2. For the history of the minting of 'Greek' coins by Hellenistic cities including Jewish cities like Tiberias and Sepphoris cf. Y.Meshorer, *City Coins of Eretz-Israel and the Decapolis in the Roman Period.* Jerusalem 1985. Only the Phoenician coastal cities kept remnants of Old Phoenician. The stylized *mem* which indicated the city God Marna(s) 'our Lord' was typical of Gaza, cf. Meshorer, *City Coins*, 29-31, with plates, and Schürer, *History* II (n.25), 62: 'The whole monetary system of Palestine was in part Phoenician-Hellenistic, and in part Greek or Roman.'

28. S.Krauss, *Griechische und lateinische Lehnwörter im Talmud, Midrasch und Targum*, I, Berlin 1898, XXX. Cf. now also *A Dictionary of Greek and Latin Terms in Rabbinic Literature* by D.Sperber, Dictionaries of Talmud, Midrash and Targum 1, Jerusalem 1984, with D.Sperber, 'Greek and Latin Words in Rabbinic Literature. Prolegomena to a New Dictionary', *Bar Ilan* 14/15, 1977, 70-8, and G.Zuntz, 'Greek Words in the Talmud', *JSS* 1, 1956, 129-40. Cf. also Schürer, *History* II (n.25), 68-73.

29. F.Perler, *Bousset's Religion des Judentums im neutestamentlichen Zeitalter kritisch untersucht*, Berlin 1903; Bousset responded with *Volksfrömmigkeit und Schriftgelehrtentum. Antwort auf Herrn Perles' Kritik meiner 'Religion des Judentums im N.T. Zeitalter'*, Berlin 1903.

30. The Copper Scroll 3Q15 (J.T.Milik, *Les 'petites grottes' de Qumran, Textes*, DJD 3, Oxford 1962, 284-99) has primarily combinations of Greek letters (Col.I, lines 4, 12; Col.II, lines 2, 4, 9; Col.III, line 7 and IV, line 2); then the terms 'peristyle' (Col.I, line 7), 'amphora' (Col.I, line 9) and finally probably even the Latin *via* in Col.V, line 13. Cf. also Schürer, *History* II (n.25), 78f.

31. The first Jewish coins with Greek images on them go back to the late Persian period. In his appendix '*Yᵉhud*-Münzen' in H.Weippert, *Palästina in vorhellenistischer Zeit*, Handbuch der Archäologie, Palästina 1, Munich 1988, 723-8, L.Mildenberg mentions a head of Pallas Athena (ibid.723 and plate 22, nos.1,3,4): the owl 'of an Athenian type' (ibid., with plate 22, nos.2-8) – it should be noted that these are official coins of the land, on which the Aramaic name of the province, *Yᵉhud*, is mentioned. According to Mildenberg (723) these coins demonstrate the cultural influence on Judaea 'in the centre' 'in a way which is as surprising as it is irrefutable'. Possibly YHWH is even

represented on these coins, see H.Kienle, *Der Gott auf dem Flügelrad*, GOF.H 7, Göttingen 1975. After the Maccabaean crisis such coins became intolerable for Jewish piety.

32. J.N.Sevenster, *Do You Know Greek? How Much Greek could the First Jewish Christians Have Known?*, NT.S 19, Leiden 1968.

33. BFCT 6, 1902, Vol.4, Gütersloh 1902, here quoted from the reprint in K.H.Rengstorf, *Johannes und sein Evangelium*, WdF 82, 1973, 30 n.1.

34. B.Isaak, 'A Donation for Herod's Temple in Jerusalem', *IEJ* 33, 1983, 86-92:

] (ἔτους) κ᾽ ἐπ᾽ ἀρχιερέως
] Πάρις Ἀκέσωνος
] ἐν Ῥόδωι Π]ροστρωσιν
δ]ραχμάς.

It is interesting that the twentieth year presumably refers to Herod and that in addition there is also mention of the high priest, though unfortunately his name has not been preserved.

35. See S.Applebaum, 'A Fragment of a New Hellenistic Inscription from the Old City of Jerusalem', in *Jerusalem in the Second Temple Period. Abraham Schalit Memorial Volume*, ed. A.Oppenheimer, U.Rappaport and M.Stern, Jerusalem 1980, 47-59, with the critical additions by B.Isaac, *SEG* 30, 1980, 1695. The riddle of the inscription is still unsolved. See now the critical judgment of B.Bar Kokhba, *Judas Maccabaeus*, Cambridge 1989, 119 n.12.

36. *CIJ* 2, 1210-1414. Sevenster, *Do You Know Greek?* (n.32), 146, counted 175 ossuary inscriptions the language on which can be determined. 64 of them are Greek, i.e. 36% (cf. *Between Jesus and Paul*, 143f. n.85). But these figures need to be increased by more recent discoveries ('What is badly needed is a systematic collection of the Greek, Aramaic and Hebrew inscriptions on ossuaries from Jerualem and elsewhere', Fitzmyer, 'Languages' [n.23], 513 n.46; such a work is now in preparation); cf. P.B.Bagatti and J.T.Milik, *Gli scavi del 'Dominus flevit'*, I.1, Jerusalem 1958, 70-109: ten Greek inscriptions, around 23%. Also *SEG* 6, 849; *SEG* 8, 179-86, 197, 201, 208f., 221, 224; *SEG* 17, 784; 19, 922; 20, 483-9; *SEG* 28, 1435; N.Avigad, *IEJ* 12, 1962, 1-12; J.Naveh, *IEJ* 20, 1970, 33-7; N.Avigad, *IEJ* 21, 1971, 185-200; E.M.Meyers, *Jewish Ossuaries: Reburial and Rebirth*, Rome 1971.

There is a new discovery relating to Acts 4.6 on an ossuary (D.Barag and D.Flusser, 'The Ossuary of Yehohanah Granddaughter of the High Priest Theophilus', *IEJ* 36, 1986, 39-44) which evidently comes from a village north of Jerusalem. The granddaugher of the high priest Theophilus (*Antt.* 18, 95, 123f., high priest between 37 and 41) was buried in it and Theophilus is mentioned on the inscription (and thus as first high priest, ibid., 41 n.8). His father Annas appears often in the New Testament (Luke 3.1; Acts 4.6; John 18.13-24; cf. Schürer, *History* II [n.25], 229). Presumably the father of the buried woman, John, is identical with the mysterious John of Acts 4.6. As the inscription is itself in *Aramaic*, but the son of Annas has a *Greek* name (*tplws*/ΘΕΟΦΙΛΟΣ) and at the same time the *Hebrew* title *hkhn hgdl* is mentioned, this is a good example of the trilinguality of the land on an inscription.

37. We find a considerable number of Greek epigrams as Jewish epitaphs in Leontopolis (Egypt), *CIJ* 2, 1451, 1489, 1490, 1508-13, 1522 and 1530, cf. *CPJ* 3, 1530a, and also two in Beth-shearim (M.Schwabe and B.Lifshitz, *Beth She'arim II: The Greek Inscriptions*, Jerusalem 1967, 127, 183) and one in Larissa (*CIJ* 1, 701): there are two Latin poems in Rome (*CIJ* 1, 476 and 527).

38. For the number of inhabitants of Jerusalem see the investigations by J.Wilkinson, 'Ancient Jerusalem, its Water Supply and Population', *PEQ* 106, 1974, 33-51, and M.Broshi, 'La population de l'ancienne Jérusalem', *RB* 82, 1975, 1-14. For both scholars the starting point is that the number had grown from 30,000 to over 80,000 between the later Hasmonaeans and 66 CE. If we take in the nearer environs including Jericho, as a rough estimate this figure seems to me to be fairly realistic.

39. N.Avigad, 'A Depository of Inscribed Ossuaries in the Kidron Valley', *IEJ* 12, 1962, 1-12 ('Alexander son of Simon, from Cyrene'). The text of the inscription runs 'Alexander, son of Simon' and has the addition *qrnyt*, which probably arises from a miswriting of *qrnyt* (*t* instead of *h*) and in that case indicates an origin in Cyrene. One of the five women mentioned there comes from Ptolemais, which similarly could point to Cyrenaica. D.Lührmann, *Das Markusevangelium*, HNT 3, Tübingen 1987, 259, thinks that the names 'Alexander' and 'Simon' are too common to establish a connection between the inscription and Mark 15.21b. Certainly there are four Alexanders and five Simons among the 532 Jewish inscriptions from Palestine in *CPJ*, but 'Alexander son of Simon' is a form of the name not so far attested and the addition *qrnyt* can meaningfully be explained as a pointer towards Cyrenaica.

40. *CIJ* 2, 1284 (Capua); *CIJ* 2, 1372-4 (Scythopolis/Beth-shean and Bethel); *CIJ* 2, 1233 mentions a Ἰοῦστος Χαλκίδηνος, who probably came from Chalcis (Antilebanon). G.Delling (*Die Bewältigung der Diasporasituation durch das hellenistische Judentum*, Berlin 1987, 38f.) attests the bond between world-wide Judaism and the 'Holy Land', which is evident in the by no means small number of Greek-speaking settlers in Jerusalem.

41. The tomb is in a collection of tombs west of the Hippodrome in Jericho. Of thirty-two inscriptions, seventeen are Greek (R.Hachlili, 'The Goliath Family in Jericho: Funerary Inscriptions from a First Century AD Jewish Monumental Tomb', *BASOR* 235, 1979, 31-70:32; for the names, ibid., 48-52; for the first mention on an inscription of a freeman who was evidently an associate member of the *familia Caesaris* see ibid., 46).

For Greek and Roman names see Schürer, *History* II (n.25), 73f. and n.249; for the Hellenistic period see my *Judaism and Hellenism* (n.16) I, 61-4.

42. *CIJ* 2, 1385 with 1230; Acts 6.9 and Tobit 1.8 (Sinaiticus).

43. F.Hüttenmeister and G.Reeg, *Die antiken Synagogen in Israel, Part 1, Die jüdischen Synagogen, Lehrhäuser und Gerichtshöfe*, Beihefte zum Tübinger Atlas des Vorderen Orients, R.B (Geisteswissenschaften) 12.1, Wiesbaden 1977, and L.Roth-Gerson, *The Greek Inscriptions from the Synagogues in Eretz Israel*, Jerusalem 1987 (in Hebrew); p.14 offers a map of synagogues divided

according to the language of their inscriptions. The inscriptions are published with a commentary in her book; see also ead., 'Similarities and Differences in Greek Synagogue Inscriptions of Eretz Israel and the Diaspora', in *Synagogues in Antiquity*, ed. A.Kasher, A.Oppenheimer and U.Rappaport, Jerusalem 1987, 133-46 (in Hebrew, with an English summary, viii). For the Hebrew and Aramaic inscriptions compare J.Naveh, *On Stone and Mosaic. The Aramaic and Hebrew Inscriptions from Ancient Synagogues*, Jerusalem 1978 (in Hebrew).

44. Hengel, *Between Jesus and Paul* (n.8), 17f. and Roth-Gerson, *Greek Inscriptions* (n.43), 76f.

45. For the conception of Jerusalem as the 'navel of the world' cf. Ezek.38.12 (LXX translates with ὀμφαλός; for the background see Ezek.5.5 and H.Schmidt, *Der heilige Fels in Jerusalem. Eine archäologische und religionsgeschichtliche Studie*, Tübingen 1933, 57f.); Jub.8.11; EthEnoch 26.1; Sib.5.520, and Josephus, *BJ* 3.52 with bSan 37a; S.Krauss, *Synagogale Altertümer*, Berlin and Vienna 1922, 194. Whereas for the Greeks the navel of the world lay in Delphi (e.g. Pindar, *Panegyrics*, 4.74f.; 6.3f.; literature in W.Fauth, 'Omphalos', *KP* 4, Munich 1979, 299; Hellenistic-Roman copies of the omphalos have been preserved on the site), for Christians the centre of the earth moved to Golgotha. This has been demonstrated with a wealth of examples by J.Jeremias ('Golgotha', *Angelos* 1, Leipzig 1926, 40-5).

46. J.Jeremias, *Jerusalem in the Time of Jesus*, London and Philadelphia 1967, 73. See below, 37f.

47. There are more popular accounts of these excavations in N.Avigad, 'Excavations in the Jewish Quarter of the Old City, 1969-1971', in *Jerusalem Revealed. Archaeology in the Holy City 1968-1974*, ed.Y.Yadin, Jerusalem 1975, 41-51, and in N.Avigad, *Discovering Jerusalem*, Nashville, Camden and New York 1983. J.Jeremias drew attention to the remains of Herodian architecture on the Temple Mount in 1942 ('Das westliche Südtor des herodianischen Tempels', first published in *ZDPV* 65, 1942, 112-18, with plates 6A and B, also in id., *Abba. Studien zur neutestamentlichen Theologie und Zeitgeschichte*, Göttingen 1966, 353-60 [with a supplement by A.M.Schneider] and Plate 4). There are detailed investigations of the temple building in his major account *Jerusalem in the Time of Jesus* (n.46 above), 21-7. There is an extended popular account by B.Mazar, *Der Berg des Herrn* (with G.Cornfeld), Bergisch Gladbach 1979, 105-19, 129-32. A cartographical and bibliographical account of all archaeological discoveries of this period is being prepared by K.Bieberstein and H.W.Bloedhorn for the *Tübinger Atlas des Vorderen Orients* (TAVO).

48. Avigad, *Discovering Jerusalem* (n.47), 95-120: stucco ceiling (ibid., 102); frescoes in the style of Pompeii II but without pictorial representations of human beings and animals (107, 150 and plates 103-195). In the Jewish Old City, however, two fragments of frescoes with representations of birds have been found (*Jerusalem Revealed*, Plate III bottom row after p.56; text, ibid., 49); according to Josephus *BJ* 5, 176-82:181, there were bronze works of art (*chalkovrēmata*) in Herod's palace in Jerusalem itself; see also M.Hengel, *The Zealots*, Edinburgh 1989, 193.

49. Avigad, *Jerusalem Revealed* (n.47), 50 (plate), 49-51 (text).

50. Jeremias, *Jerusalem* (n.46), 6-16; or N.Avigad, 'The Architecture of Jerusalem in the Second Temple Period', in *Jerusalem Revealed* (n.47), 14-20: 17-20.
The technical standard of the Herodian buildings is indicated by the discoveries which have been made in various excavations in Jerusalem over recent years; in addition to Avigad, 'Excavations in the Jewish Quarter' (n.47) see id., *Discovering Jerusalem* (n.47), 88. It is worth noting the high level of artistic production in Jerusalem or the importation of precious works of art from abroad. Thus for example an artistic glass jug has been found in Jerusalem with the Greek inscription ENNIΩN EΠOIEI (Avigad, *Discovering Jerusalem*, 88, plates 95f.). It is evidently the product of a workshop supervised by Ennion; glass from this workshop has been preserved from a variety of places in the Mediterranean (cf. D.Whitehouse in *Glas der Caesaren*, ed. D.B.Harden, H.Hellenkemper, K.Painter and D.Whitehouse, catalogue of the 1988 Cologne exhibition, 164-6, with illustrations of two vessels). Avigad discovered traces of a glass-blowing workshop from the time of Alexander Jannaeus in the present Jewish quarter of the Old City of Jerusalem (N.Avigad, 'Excavations in the Jewish Quarter of the Old City in Jerusalem, 1971 (Third Preliminary Report)', *IEJ* 22, 1972, 193-200: 199f.).

51. G.Delling, *Die Bewältigung der Diasporasituation durch das hellenistische Judentum*, Berlin 1987, 36; Cicero engages in polemic in *pro Flacco* 67 against the outflow of money to Jerusalem (*Greek and Latin Authors on Jews and Judaism*, ed. with Introductions, Translations and Commentary by M.Stern, Publications of the Israel Academy of Sciences and Humanities. Section of Humanities. Fontes ad Res Judaicas Spectantes, Vol.1, *From Herodotus to Plutarch*, Jerusalem 1974 [= *GLAJ*], no.66, 198-201; see Delling, *Bewältigung*, with nn.220-4 and bibliography).

52. See Hengel, *Zealots* (n.48), 206-10; Jeremias, *Jerusalem in the Time of Jesus* (n.46), 49, 174f.

53. M.Ben-Dov, *In the Shadow of the Temple. The Discovery of Ancient Jerusalem*, New York 1985, 149-67.

54. Pausanias, 8.16.4f. (text and English translation in *GLAJ*, Vol.2, *From Tacitus to Simplicius*, Jerusalem 1980, no.358, pp.196f.), for Queen Helena see Josephus, *Antt.*20.95 and M.Stern's commentary (ibid., 197). For the building see also M.Kon (= Cohen), *The Tombs of the Kings*, Tel Aviv 1947 (Hebrew) and Schürer, *History* (n.25) III, 163f.

55. Suetonius, *Nero* 40.2; *Augustus* 93 differs (conveniently accessible in *GLAJ*, Vol.2, no.303, p.110); Polybius,16.39.1,4 = Josephus, *Antt.* 12.136 (*GLAJ*, Vol.1, no.32, pp.113-15); Numenius, Frag.56 (*Numénius, Fragments, texte établi et traduit par E. des Places*, CUFr, Paris 1973, 100 [= Lydus, *Mens.*4.53, *GLAJ*, Vol.2, no.367, p.215]) and a Livy quotation from the scholia on Lucan (ed. H.Usener, 2,593, *GLAJ*, Vol.1, no.133, p.300; cf. Lucan, *Pharsalia* 2.590-4 = *GLAJ*, Vol.1, no.191, p.439); cf. Josephus, BJ 6.123,260; Dio Cassius 66.5.2; 6.2 (*GLAJ* 2, no.430, pp.372f.).

56. Jeremias, *Jerusalem in the Time of Jesus* (n.46), 77-83; Schürer, *History*

(n.25) II, 76; in Jeremias there is also information about the economic significance of the pilgrim traffic (134-8).

57. Cf.above with nn.47-50; also A.Schalit, *König Herodes. Der Mann und sein Werk*, SJ 4, Berlin 1969, 328-403, and Schürer, *History* (n.25) II, 304-9; now also H.Merkel, 'Herodes der Grosse A.-D.', in *RAC* 14, Stuttgart 1988, 815-30: 820-2.

58. Text e.g. in *CIJ* 2, 1404; text and translation also in *Between Jesus and Paul* (n.8), 17f.; for the 'Synagogue of the Libertines' see ibid. and 148 n.116.

59. See Schürer, *History* (n.25) II, 76 and n.256; Hengel, *Between Jesus and Paul* (n.8), 16f.

60. See the information in the Theodotus inscription that the synagogue is εἰς ἀν[άγν]ωσ[ιν] νόμου καὶ εἰς [δ]ιδαχ[ὴ]ν ἐντολῶν, see my *Between Jesus and Paul* (n.8), 17f. with 148 nn.119,122.

61. H.Conzelmann, *The Acts of the Apostles*, Hermeneia, Philadelphia 1987, 68.

62. Josephus, *Antt.* 15.320ff.; 17.78; for the family there are examples in my *Judaism and Hellenism* (n.16) II, 53 n.156; for the Boethusians, R.Meyer, Σαδδυκαῖος, *TDNT* 7, Grand Rapids 1971, 35-54: 42f., 45f., and Schürer, *History* (n.25) II, 229 and n.53. Herod married a daughter of Simon son of Boethus (Josephus, *Antt.* 15, 320f.), but disinherited her son Herod. For the luxury of the family see Jeremias, *Jerusalem* (n.46), 97. The rabbinic tradition knows of the fabulous riches of Martha, daughter of the high priest Boethus, who married the high priest Jehoshua B.Gamla; (H.L.Strack and) P.Billerbeck, *Kommentar zum Neuen Testament aus Talmud und Midrasch* 2, Munich ⁸1983, 184f., and L.Ginzberg, 'Boethusians (*bytwsym*)', *JE* 3, London and New York 1902, 284f.

63. *CIJ* 1, 1256; cf. E.Bammel, 'Nicanor and his Gate', first published in *JJS* 7, 1956, 77f., in id., *Judaica*, Kleine Schriften 1, WUNT 37, Tübingen 1986, 39-41: similarly J.P.Kane, 'Ossuary Inscriptions of Jerusalem', *JJS* 23, 1978, 279-82; also my 'Luke the Historian and the Geography of Palestine in the Acts of the Apostles', in *Between Jesus and Paul* (n.8), 97-128: 102ff.

64. Schürer, *History* II (n.25), 57f. n.170.

65. According to mGitt 9.8 a letter of divorce is also valid with Greek signatures, cf. also Schürer, *History* II, 79f.

66. S.Applebaum, 'Hellenistic Cities of Judea and its Vicinity – Some New Aspects', in *The Ancient Historian and his Materials. Essays in honour of G.E.Stevens on his 70th Birthday*, ed. B.Levick, 1975, 59-73, gives a survey of the Hellenistic cities in Judaea; see also what is by far the best account in Schürer, *History* II (n.25), 85-183.

For Caesarea, we have in Josephus (*BJ* 2.457) the information that in the pogroms at the beginning of the Jewish War in 66 CE 20,000 Jews were killed, and also that the Jewish population had previously been organized as an independent *politeuma* and had fought for a long time previously with the Greek population for equal political rights in the city (Schürer, *History* I [n.25], 164, 465, 467; II, 183). Cf. L.I.Levine, *Caesarea under Roman Rule*, SJLA 7, Leiden 1975, 22f.; for the location of the Jewish quarter of the city see id.,

'Roman Caesarea. An Archaeological-Topographical Study', *Qedem* 2, 1975, 40-5; also Applebaum, 'Hellenistic Cities', 61; for the population see J.Ringel, *Césarée du Palestine. Étude Historique et Archéologique*, Paris 1975, Chapter II, 'Le Problème Démographique', 88-92. Applebaum (67) mentions fragments of sculpture which illustrate the artistic level in the city; cf. C.Vermeule and K.Anderson, 'Greek and Roman Sculpture in the Holy Land', *Burlington Magazine* 123, no.934, 1981, 7-19; there, however, the fragment of a statue which has been identified as that of Zeus has been dated to the time of Trajan or Hadrian (11). For the investigation of the harbour in Caesarea built by Herod see now also R.L.Hohlfelder, J.P.Oleson, A.Raban and R.L.Vann, 'Sebastos. Herod's Harbour at Caesarea Maritima', *BA* 46, 1983, 133-43. It improved the exchange of goods and the transport of pilgrims; luxury goods, too, were now easier to bring into the country. Thus wine from the Aegean was known from the third century BCE onwards (see below). However, Herod supplied himself with Italian wine, perhaps from his own vineyard: inscribed amphorae discovered in Masada contained 'Philonianum' wine, which probably came from Brindisi (*Jerusalem Post*, 10 May 1986, 22). There is a good survey of Caesarea in Schürer, *History* II (n.25), 115-18.

For Ashdod cf. Josephus, *BJ* 4.130: there was evidently a significant Jewish population in the city, which belonged to Judaea under Alexander Jannaeus (103-76 BCE, *Antt.* 13.395) and was then detached from it again by Pompey (*BJ* 1.156, 166; cf. also Acts 8.40); cf. Schürer, *History* II (n.25), 108f.

For Jamnia cf. Strabo 16.2.28 (in *GLAJ* 1, no.114, pp.290-4, with commentary). Philo exaggeratedly calls the city 'the most populous city of Judaea' (*Leg. Gai.* 200); he also attests that the majority of the population was Jewish. Jamnia (Jabneh) remained Jewish even after 70 and became the setting of the school of Johanan b.Zakkai, who consolidated Palestinian Judaism from there (Schürer, *History* I, 524-6; also J.Neusner, 'The Formation of Rabbinic Judaism: Yavneh (Jamnia) from A.D.70 to 100', *ANRW* II.19.2, *Religion* (*Judentum: Allgemeines; Palästinisches Judentum*), ed W.Haase, Berlin and New York 1979, 3-42, and P.Schäfer, 'Die Flucht Johanan ben Zakkais aus Jerusalem und die Gründung des "Lehrhauses" in Jabne', *ANRW* II.19.2, 43-101).

H.-P.Kuhnen, *Nordwestpalästina in hellenistisch-römischer Zeit. Bauten und Gräber im Karmelgebiet*, Quellen und Forschungen zur prähistorischen und provinzialrömischen Archäologie 1, Weinheim 1987, has shown that the lavish development of Caesarea probably led to a decline in the density of settlement in the area of Carmel (72f.). Perhaps there was a synoecism here similar to that later at the foundation of Tiberias by Herod Antipas. Kuhnen also describes the economic consequences of 'Hellenization', ibid., 74-7.

67. Hengel, 'Luke the Historian', in *Between Jesus and Paul* (n.8), 111-16.

68. Cf.B.Lifshitz, 'Césarée de Palestine, son histoire et ses institutions', *ANRW* II.8 (n.3), 490-518.

69. 'Luke the Historian' in *Between Jesus and Paul* (n.8), 123f.; cf. also Schürer, *History* II (n.25), 145-8; for the legal situation in the Decapolis generally see ibid. 125f. (on Pella); 160-4 (on Samaria-Sebaste, the population

of which was without doubt predominantly pagan, ibid.16); according to this passage a substantial number of Jews lived in Scythopolis, but they nevertheless formed a minority, cf. ibid., 142-5; for Tiberias and Sepphoris see ibid., 178-82 and 172-6 respectively and below, p.39.

70. For Galilee cf. E.M.Meyers, 'The Cultural Setting of Galilee: The Case of Regionalism and Early Judaism', *ANRW* II.19.1, Berlin and New York 1979, 686-702; S.Freyne, *Galilee from Alexander the Great to Hadrian, 323 BCE to 135 CE. A Study of Second Temple Judaism*, University of Notre Dame. Center for the Study of Judaism and Christianity in Antiquity 5, Notre Dame 1980, and now id., *Galilee, Jesus and the Gospels. Literary Approaches and Historical Investigations*, Dublin 1988; for Tiberias in addition to Schürer, *History*, see M.Avi-Yonah, 'The Foundation of Tiberias', *IEJ* 1, 1950/51, 160-9; for Sepphoris see also H.W.Hoehner, *Herod Antipas*, Cambridge 1972, 84; also R.Vale, 'Literary Sources in Archaeological Description: The Case of Galilee, Galilees and Galileans', *JSJ* 18, 1987, 209-26.

71. In addition to Schürer, H.Bietenhard, 'Die Dekapolis von Pompeius bis Trajan. Ein Kapitel aus der neutestamentlichen Zeitgeschichte', *ZDPV* 79, 1963, 24-7; id., 'Die syrische Dekapolis von Pompeius bis Trajan', *ANRW* II.8 (n.3), 220-61; also A.Spickermann, *The Coins of the Decapolis and Provincia Arabia*, SBF.CMa 25, ed. with historical and geographical introductions by M.Piccirillo, Jerusalem 1980, and F.G.Lang, 'Über Tyros und Sidon mitten ins Gebiet der Dekapolis', *ZDPV* 94, 1978, 145-60.

For the history of settlement cf. also S.Applebaum, 'Jewish Urban Communities and Greek Influences', *Scripta Classica Israelica* 5, 1979/80, 158-77.

72. For Scythopolis cf. M.Avi-Yonah, 'Skythopolis', *IEJ* 12, 1962, 123-36, and B.Lifshitz, 'Scythopolis. L'histoire, les institutions et les cultes de la ville à l'époque hellénistique et impériale', *ANRW* II.8 (n.3), 262-94, with G.Foerster and V.Tsafrir, 'Nysa-Scythopolis – A New Inscription and the Titles of the City on the Coins', *Israel Numismatic Journal* 9, 1986-7, 53-8. For Gaba see Josephus, *BJ* 2.459; 3.36; *Antt.* 15.294; *Vita* 115-118; G.Schmitt, 'Gaba, Cotta und Gintikirmil', *ZDPV* 103, 1987, 22-48; Schürer, *History* II (n.25), 164f.

73. E.Schürer, *Geschichte des jüdischen Volkes im Zeitalter Jesu Christi* 2, Leipzig ³1898, 135 and n.293, still differed.

74. Pliny, 5.18.74: '*Scythopolim, antea Nysam, a Libero Patre sepulta nutrice ibi Scythis deductis.*'

75. Cf. e.g. Herodotus 4.46 and O.Michel, Σκύθης, *TDNT* 7, Grand Rapids 1971, 447-50.

76. M.Hengel, 'The Interpretation of the Wine Miracle at Cana: John 2.1-11', in *The Glory of Christ in the New Testament. Studies in Christology in Memory of G.B.Caird*, ed. L.D.Hurst and N.T.Wright, Oxford 1987, 83-112.

77. R.Talgam and Z.Weiss, ' "The Dionysus Cycle" in the Sepphoris Mosaic', *Qad.* 21, 1988, 93-9 (in Hebrew).

78. G.Fuks, 'Tel Anafa – A Proposed Identification', *Scripta Classica Israelica* 5, 1979/80, 178-84, has proposed the identification of Tell Anafa (Tell el-Ahdar, about six miles south of Caesarea Philippi) with Arsinoe in Coele Syria, a city known from the *Ethnica* of Stephen of Byzantium (ed. A.Meinecke,

Berlin 1849, 125, reissued Graz 1958). Epigraphic material and ceramics indicate that there was a Hellenistic city on the tell. See already S.Weinberg, 'Tel Anafa: The Hellenistic Town', *IEJ* 21, 1971, 86-109.

79. H.G.Liddell, R.Scott and H.S.Jones, *A Greek-English Lexicon*, Oxford ⁹1940, s.v., 1758.

80. Schürer, *History* I (n.25), 144, 228 n.31; on Tarichaea see ibid., I, 494f. n.44 and II, 193f. n.43.

81. M.Schwabe and B.Lifshitz, *Beth She'arim II: The Greek Inscriptions*, Jerusalem 1967, contains 218 Greek inscriptions; by contrast there are only 28 in Hebrew or Aramaic (*Beth She'arim III: Report on the Excavations during 1953-1958*, Vol.III, by N.Avigad, Jerusalem 1976, 230-54 and *Beth She'arim I: Report on the Excavations 1936-1940*, Vol.I, by B.Mazar, Jerusalem 1976, 193-206).

82. *Sammelbuch griechischer Urkunden aus Ägypten* (*SGU*) 8, 9843: Ἐγράφη δ[ὲ] Ἑλληνιστὶ διὰ τ[ὸ ὁρ]μᾶν μὴ εὑρηθῆ[ῆ]ναι Ἑβραεστὶ γ[ρα]φασθαι' ('The letter was written in Greek because we have no one here capable of writing Hebrew'): first published by B.Lifshitz, 'Papyrus Grecs du désert de Juda', *Aeg* 42, 1962, 240-56; cf. Fitzmyer, 'Languages of Palestine' (n.23), 514f.; he interprets the signature 'Soumaoios' under the letter quoted as possibly that of Shim'on bar Kosibah and provides text and an English translation. A further Greek letter from a leader under Bar Kosiba at the feast of Tabernacles has the usual Greek letter-prescript (as, too, does James 1.1): '[Ἀ]ννανος Ἰωναθῆ τῶι ἀδελφῷ χαίρειν', *SGU* 8, 9844; cf. Schürer, *History* II (n.25), 28 n.118, and ibid., 79 with n.279; also M.Hengel, 'Der Jakobusbrief als antipaulinische Polemik', in *Tradition and Interpretation in the New Testament. Essays in Honor of E.Earle Ellis*, ed. G.F.Hawthorne with O.Betz, Grand Rapids, Michigan and Tübingen 1987, 248-78: 251, 270 with n.31.

83. Cf.H.P.Rüger, 'Die lexikalischen Aramaismen im Markusevangelium', in *Markusphilologie. Historische, literarische und stilistische Untersuchungen zum zweiten Evangelium*, ed.H.Cancik, WUNT 33, Tübingen 1984, 73-84. The list of fifteen Jewish Christian bishops of Jerusalem which Eusebius hands down in HE 4.5.3 contains two Latin names (Justus and Seneca) and the Greek name Philip; however, the tradition of these names is shaky (A.von Harnack, *Geschichte der altchristlichen Literatur bis Eusebius*, 2.1, Leipzig 1897, reissued 1958, 220f. n.3) and it is uncertain how far one can rely historically on the various traditions (on this see most recently R.van den Broek, 'Der Brief des Jakobus an Quadratus und das Problem der judenchristlichen Bischöfe von Jerusalem', in *Text and Testimony. Essays on New Testament and Apocryphal Literature in Honour of A.F.J.Klijn*, ed.T.Baarda et al., Kampen 1988, 56-65).

84. Luke always has Simon for Shim'on (Peter; cf. e.g. Acts 10.5); only in Acts 15.14 does he put a Συμεών on the lips of James the brother of the Lord. II Peter 1.1 has the pseudepigraphically archaizing Συμεὼν Πέτρος.

85. Josephus, *Antt.* 18.28; the reason given there is the large number of inhabitants; cf. the suggestion for a location by B.Pixner, 'Searching for the New Testament Site of Bethsaida', *BA* 48, 1985, 207-16; cf. also Schürer, *History* II (n.25), 176-8.

86. The same goes for the Jewish officer Philip son of Jakimos, mentioned

by Josephus in *BJ* 2.421 or 556 and *Vita* 46-61, the commander of Agrippa II's cavalry, from Batanaea.

87. Hengel, 'Luke the Historian', in *Between Jesus and Paul* (n.8), 105f., 119f.

88. M.Hengel, 'The Gospel of Mark: Time of Origin and Situation', in *Studies in the Gospel of Mark*, London and Philadelphia 1985, 1-30 and 117-38: 29 and 138 n.164. There, on the other hand, one could presuppose a knowledge of Phoenician-Canaanite, which was closely related to Hebrew. F.Millar, 'Empire, Community and Culture' (n.3), 149, gives an example of how even in the late Roman period citizens in Gaza with a Greek upbringing could speak the Aramaic vernacular.

89. R.A.Batey, 'Is not this the Carpenter?', *NTS* 30, 1984, 249-58.

90. B.Schwank even thinks it possible that the family of Jesus visited the theatre in Sepphoris ('Das Theater von Sepphoris und die Jugendjahre Jesu', *EuA* 52, 1976, 199-206). But it seems to me very doubtful whether one may assume this in the case of a Jewish family of strict observance. Nor can I fully agree with R.A.Batey that 'there was no apparent reason for a young man from Nazareth to avoid this city'. As Jesus came from a pious Jewish craftsman's family, with country origins, there are reasons which tell *against* too close a connection with the largely Hellenistic city in the vicinity after its reconstruction. Moreover the dating of the theatre is disputed. B.Schwank ('Die neuen Ausgrabungen in Sepphoris', *BiKi* 42, 1987, 75-9) reports the conjecture of excavators in 1985 that the theatre was built in the first century (E.M.Meyers, E.Netzer, C.L.Meyers, 'Sepphoris – "Ornament of all Galilee"', *BA* 49, 1986, 4-19). However, in 1983 Batey shifted the construction of the theatre into the second century ('Jesus and the Theatre', *NTS* 30, 1984, 563-74), only to contradict his dating later (id., 'Subsurface Interface Radar at Sepphoris, Israel, 1985', *Journal of Field Archaeology* 14, 1987, 1-8, here 2f.). He too now puts the building of the theatre in the first century BCE (cf. also J.F.Strange, T.R.W.Longstaff, 'Sepphoris (Sippori)', *IEJ* 34, 1984, 51f., and J.F.Strange, 'Chronique Archéologique: Sepphoris et autres sites de basse Galilée', *RB* 91, 1984, 239-41). It is at any rate striking that the Gospel tradition does not mention Sepphoris at all. (This could be explained in terms of territorial history, in view of the proximity of Nazareth, thus A.Alt, 'Die Stätten des Wirkens Jesu in Galiläa territorialgeschichtlich betrachtet', *Kleine Schriften* II, Munich ²1959, 436-56). However, Tiberias is mentioned in John 6.23 (cf.6.1; 21.1, see below, 39).

91. T.Zahn, *Einleitung in das Neue Testament*, Leipzig ³1906, 31, 79; Sevenster, *Do You Know Greek?* (n.32), 15; now Hengel, 'Jakobusbrief als Polemik' (n.82), 270 n.33 and 281.

92. E.W.Dinkler, 'Der Brief an die Galater – Zum Kommentar von H.Schlier', first published in *Verkündigung und Forschung. Theologischer Jahresbericht*, 1953/55, now in id., *Signum Crucis. Aufsätze zum Neuen Testament und zur Christlichen Archäologie*, Tübingen 1967, 270-82, esp.280; G.Klein, 'Galater 2, 6-9 und die Geschichte der Jerusalemer Urgemeinde', first published in *ZTK* 57, 1960, 275-95, in id., *Rekonstruktion und Interpretation. Gesammelte Aufsätze zum Neuen Testament*, BEvTh 50, Munich 1969, 99-118, with supplement 118-28;

for the question of the protocol, 118-20. The remarkable 'Petros' (instead of Cephas) in Gal.2.7 already tells against this: if Paul is quoting from a protocol at all, it is from a *Greek* protocol which was common to all.

93. Acts 13.1; Philippus Sidetes, *HE*, fragment in Codex Baroccianus 142, ed.C.de Boer, TU 5.2, 170; now conveniently accessible with a translation in U.H.J.Körtner, *Papias von Hierapolis. Ein Beitrag zur Geschichte des frühen Christentums*, FRLANT 133, Göttingen 1983, 63f.

94. Ibid.

95. Mark 15.21; cf. Rom.16.13. Here it is presupposed that the Gospel was written in Rome (Hengel, 'Gospel of Mark: Time of Origin' [n.8], 28) and that the Rufus mentioned in Romans is identical with Simon's son (cf. J.Gnilka, *Das Evangelium nach Markus: Mk 8,27-16.20*, EKK 2.2, Zürich, Einsiedeln, Cologne and Neukirchen-Vluyn 1979, 315).

96. For the 'Seven' see *Between Jesus and Paul* (n.8), 13; for Paul see my study on the pre-Christian Paul in *Paulus. Missionar und Theologe und das antike Judentum*, WUNT, Tübingen, forthcoming.

97. H.I.Marrou, *Histoire de l'éducation dans l'antiquité*, Paris 1948, 145.

98. Ben Sira's grandson renders the Hebrew *musar* as παιδεία, cf. R.Smend, *Griechisch-Syrisch-Hebräischer Index zur Weisheit des Jesus Sirach*, Berlin 1907, 176f.; for the Jewish school see my *Judaism and Hellenism* (n.16), I, Excursus 1, 78-82.

99. Millar, 'Empire, Community and Culture' (n.3), 147.

100. On this see my article 'Qumran und der Hellenismus', in *Qumran. Sa piété, sa théologie, et son milieu*, ed. M.Delcor, BETL 46, Paris and Louvain 1978, 333-72.

101. See my *Judaism and Hellenism* (n.16), with literature on Menippus, II, 56 n.196.

102. Meleager's recollection of Gadara was vivid, although he probably did not see his home town again; in *Anthologia Graeca* 5,160 (LCL, *Greek Anthology*, ed.W.R.Paton, I, 1916, p.205.; *G LAJ*, Vol.I, no.43, p.140), he laments that his beloved Demo is warming herself on the cold sabbath with her Jewish lover: σαββατικὸς... πόθος and ψυχροῖς σάββασι. Agatharcides, two generations earlier, mentions only the 'seventh day', Josephus, *c.Apionem* 1.209. This is perhaps the first mention of the Jewish sabbath by a pagan author; for the literary motive see Stern, 140. J.Geiger, 'Greek in the Talmud: An Allusion to a Hellenistic Epigram', *Tarbiz* 55, 1988, 606f., conjectures that there is an allusion to this epigram of Meleager's in bShab 62b-63a.

103. Hengel, *Judaism and Hellenism* (n.16) I, 186 and II, 90f. n.215 with bibliography. For the library see M.Gigante, 'La biblioteca di Filodemo', *Cronache Ercolanei* 15, 1985, 5-30.

104. Suetonius, *Tiberius*, 57. The author of the work Περὶ Ὕψους was possibly a pupil of his (see Hengel, *Judaism and Hellenism* [n.16], I, 260): at any rate he was not Longinus (thus also R.Brandt, *Pseudo-Longinus. Vom Erhabenen*, Texte zur Forschung 37, Darmstadt ²1983, 11f.).

105. See H.J.Mette, *PRE* 17.2, Stuttgart 1937, 2249-51, and my *Judaism and Hellenism* (n.16), I, 83 and II, 56 n.189 (with examples and literature); also

L.Blau, 'Oenomaus of Gadara', *JE* 9, New York and London 1905, 385f.; D.Sperber, 'Oenomaus of Gadara', *EJ* 12, Jerusalem 1971, 1331f., with Schürer, *History* II (n.25), 50, 135.

106. Cf. Eusebius, *Preparatio Evangelica* 5.21.6 (GCS Eusebius Werke 8, ed.Mras/des Places 1,262); 5.36.5 (1,290): the fourteen surviving fragments, which have been preserved only by Eusebius, are conveniently indicated in the index to the Berlin edition, ibid.2, 452f.

107.'...πάτρα δέ με τεκνοῖ
'Ατθὶς ἐν 'Ασσυρίοις ναιομένα Γαδάροις': 'but Gadara was my homeland/ that new Athens in the land of the Assyrians (*Anthologia Graeca* 7,417.1f., LCL, ed.Paton (n.102), 2, p.225..

108. Liddell-Scott-Jones, *Lexicon* (n.79), Supplement 151 (= R.Perdrizet, *Revue d'Archéologie*, 3ᵉᵐᵉ Sér. 35, 1899, 49f.: 'ville lettrée', see Hengel, *Judaism and Hellenism* (n.16), I, 83 and II, 56 n.194; Schürer, *History* II (n.25), 153f. n.255 (with more recent literature).

109. Stephen of Byzantium, *Ethnica*, ed. A.Meinecke, Berlin 1849, 203 (reprinted Graz 1958).

110. For Ashkelon, in addition to Schürer, *History* II (n.5), 49-51, see also M.Hengel, 'Rabbinische Legende und frühpharisäische Geschichte. Schimeon b.Schetach und die achtzig Hexen von Askalon', *AHAW.PH* 2, 1984, Heidelberg 1984, 41-4.

111. Stephen of Byzantium, *Ethnica* (n.109), 132. The source is probably Herennius Philo of Byblos; cf. also Strabo 16.2.29 (759). Stephen mentions the Stoics Sosus, Antibius and Eubius, and also as grammarians Ptolemaeus, Aristarchus and Dorotheus with the historians Apollonius and Artemidorus.

112. *Aristeas* 48, 121 (knowledge of Greek and Jewish literature; Greek names); cf. Delling, *Bewältigung der Diasporasituation* (n.40), 67 n.447; Philo, *Vit.Mos.* 2.25-40 (ed.L.Cohn 4, 206.1-209.17); Meg 9a Bar; cf. tractate Sopherim 1.8.

113. 7Q 1.1-2 (= Exodus 28.4-6,7); 7Q 2.1 (= EpJer 43), in *Exploration de falaise, les Grottes 2Q,3Q,4Q,5Q,6Q,7Q à 10Q*, ed. M.Baillet, J.T.Milik, R.de Vaux, DJD 3, *Les 'petites grottes de Qumran'*, Oxford 1962, 142f.; cf. also Schürer, *History* II (n.25), 78. There is more literature on the subject there.

114. 'Les grottes de Murabbaʿat', ed. P.Benoit, J.T.Milik, R.de Vaux, DJD 3.3, *Textes Grecs et Latins*, 207-77. Cf. also Schürer, *History* II (n.25), 78f. In Nahal Hever papyri were found from the time of the Bar Kochba revolt, most of them written in Greek and coming from the family archive of the Jewish woman Babatha, daughter of Simon. Of 35 documents 6 are in Nabataean, 3 in Aramaic, 17 in Greek and 9 in Greek with Nabataean or Aramaic signatures (Y.Yadin, *Bar Kokhba: The Rediscovery of the Legendary Hero of the Last Jewish Revolt against Imperial Rome*, London and New York 1971, 229; so far only three of the Greek texts have been published: *SGU* 10,10288,1-3 [first by H.J.Polotsky, 'Three Greek Documents from the Family Archive of Babata', *ErIs* 8, 1967, 46-51, in Hebrew], and N.Lewis, *Two Greek Documents from Provincia Arabia*, Illinois Classical Studies 3, 1978, 100-14). Babatha's Greek marriage contract (Papyrus Yadin 18), which was concluded according

to *Greek law*, has now also been published: N.Lewis, R.Katzoff and J.C.Green-field, 'Papyrus Yadin 18', *IEJ* 37, 1987, 229-50. In a tax matter the woman swears to her information 'by the Tyche of Lord Caesar' (Yadin, *Bar Kokhba*, 246).

115. Göttingen LXX siglum 943; it was probably written in the middle of the first century CE; cf. S.P.Brock, 'Bibelübersetzungen I.2. Die Übersetzungen des Alten Testaments ins Griechische', *TRE* 6, Berlin and New York 1980, 163-72: 164; also D.Barthélemy, 'Redécouverte d'un chaînon manquant de l'histoire de la Septante', first published in *RB* 60, 1953, 18-29; in id., *Études d'histoire du Texte de l'Ancien Testament*, OBO 21, Fribourg and Göttingen 1978, 38-50.

116. On this see the thorough investigation by D.A.Koch, *Die Schrift als Zeuge des Evangeliums. Untersuchungen zur Verwendung und zum Verständnis der Schrift bei Paulus*, BHT 69, Tübingen 1986, 48-87. Koch, however, thinks that Paul completely failed to notice that he was using a divergent text (81), and tends to underestimate Paul's knowledge of scripture (92ff.), so that his picture is questionable (cf. also the review by H.Hübner, *TLZ* 113, 1988, 349-52).

117. Eusebius, *Praeparatio Evangelica* 9.17 and 18.2 (= *FGrH* 3C no.724). Cf. my *Judaism and Hellenism* (n.16) I, 88-92; A.M.Denis, *Introduction aux pseudépigraphes grecs d'Ancien Testament*, Leiden 1970, 261; T.Rajak, 'The Sense of History in Jewish Intertestamental Writing', *OTS* 24, 1986, 124-45: 139f.; D.Mendels, *The Land of Israel as Political Concept in Hasmonaean Literature*, TSAJ 15, Tübingen 1987, 116-19. The author was certainly a Samaritan (see Schürer, *History* III [n.25], 528-30, and my review 'Der alte und der neue "Schürer"', *JSS* 1990, forthcoming).

118. I Macc.12.6ff.; Josephus, *Antt.* 12.226f.; 13.167f.; cf. also II Macc.5 and my *Judaism and Hellenism* (n.16) I, 72; B.Cardauns, 'Juden und Spartaner. Zur hellenistisch-jüdischen Literatur', *Hermes* 95, 1967, 317-24; E.(J.)Bickerman, 'Origines Gentium', first published in *CP* 47, 1952, 65-81, in id., *Religions and Politics in the Hellenistic and Roman Periods*, ed. E.Gabba and M.Smith, Bibliotheca di Athenaeum 5, Como 1985, 401-17. Another tradition knows of friendship between Abraham and the Pergamenes (Josephus, *Antt.*14.255).

119. J.Jeremias, 'ΙΕΡΟΥΣΑΛΗΜ/ΙΕΡΟΣΟΛΥΜΑ', *ZNW* 65, 1972, 273-6; R.Schütz, 'Ιερουσαλημ und Ιεροσολυμα im Neuen Testament', *ZNW* 11, 1910, 169-87; cf. my *Jews, Greeks and Barbarians* (n.23), 119f. For the short form ΣΟΛΥΜΑ/ΟΙΣ add: Sib.4.115, 126; cf.12.103; Tacitus, *Hist.* 5.2.3 (*GLAJ*, ed.Stern, Vol.2, no.281, p.18); Philostratus, *VA* 5.27 (*GLAJ*, Vol.2, no.402, p.340); 6.29,34 (no.404a/b, pp.342f.); Pausanias 8.16.5 (*GLAJ*, Vol.2, no.358, p.196); there are further instances in Stern's index under Solyma (*GLAJ*, Vol.3, 149). Pagan writers may sometimes be using the word in order to avoid the Ἱερο, which they feel inappropriate. In Latin poetry Solyma is customary (thus M.Stern on no.402 [see above], *GLAJ*, Vol.2, 340). When Vespasian besieged τὰ Σόλυμα, Philostratus refused to visit him there because the Jewish territory had been made unclean by the actions and sufferings of its inhabitants. The honourable designation which was originally orientated on Homer ultimately takes on a negative character as a result of anti-Judaism.

120. II Macc.4.9-14; I Macc.1.14f.; cf. Josephus, *Antt.* 12.251; Hengel, *Judaism and Hellenism* (n.16) I, 70-6, 304-9. K.Bringmann, *Hellenistische Reform und Religionsverfolgung in Judäa. Eine Untersuchung zur jüdisch-hellenistischen Geschichte (175-163 v. Chr.)*, AAWG.PH 132, 1983, 22ff., does not take the religious monstrosity of these events in Jerusalem for the Jewish theocracy seriously enough. He therefore arrives at an incorrect overall assessment; see also the critical discussion by T.Fischer, 'Zu einer Untersuchung der jüdisch-hellenistischen Geschichte', *Klio* 67, 1985, 350-5, here especially 352, and S.Applebaum, *Gnomon* 57, 1985, 191-3.

121. Such an export of writing can be seen in the colophon of the Greek book of Esther, cf. below 24 and n.131.

122. B.Z.Wacholder, *Eupolemus. A Study of Judaeo-Greek Literature*, Monographs of the Hebrew Union College 3, Cincinnati, New York, Los Angeles and Jerusalem 1974; cf. Schürer, *History* III (n.25), 517-21, and Mendels, *The Land of Israel* (n.117), 29-46, with Rajak, 'The Sense of History' (n.117), 137f.

123. Wacholder, *Eupolemus* (n.122), 259-306.

124. Hengel, *Judaism and Hellenism* (n.16) I, 95-9; Schürer, *History* (n.16) III, 531-7; C.Habicht, *2.Makkabäerbuch*, JSHRZ 1.3, Gütersloh [2]1979; cf. II Macc.2.21; 4.25; 5.22; 10.4; 13.9; 15.2.

125. Josephus, *Vita* 2; cf. Fitzmyer, 'Languages of Palestine' (n.23), 510f. (on *Antt.*20.263-5).

126. Josephus, *Vita* 16. Cf. on his education Schürer, *History* (n.25) I,43f. and the literature mentioned in L.H.Feldman, *Josephus and Modern Scholarship (1937-1980)*, Berlin and New York 1984, 79-84, 803-38; see also T.Rajak, *Josephus. The Historian and his Society*, London and Phildelphia 1983, 11-45, 46-64; P.Bilde, *Flavius Josephus between Jerusalem and Rome*, JSPseudepigrapha Suppl.Series 2, Sheffield 1988, 28ff., 200ff.

127. Photius, Bibl.cod.33 (*Photius, Bibliothèque*, Tome I ['Codices' 184], Text and translation by R.Henry, CUFr, Paris 1959, 18f.): *FGrH* 3 C no.734 (the title was probably περὶ Ἰουδαίων βασιλέων τῶν ἐν τοῖς στέμμασιν, cf. Schürer, *History* I (n.16), 34-7, with A.Barzanò, 'Giusto di Tiberiade', *ANRW* 20, *Hellenistisches Judentum in römischer Zeit: Allgemeines*, Berlin and New York 1987, 337-58; T.Rajak, 'Justus of Tiberias', *CQ* 23, 1973, 345-68; id., 'Josephus and Justus of Tiberias', in *Josephus, Judaism and Christianity*, ed.L.H.Feldman and G.Hata, Leiden 1987, 81-94.

128. Wacholder, *Eupolemus* (n.122), 300f.

129. E.Haenchen, *The Gospel of John*, ed.R.W.Funk and U.Busse, Hermeneia, Philadelphia 1980, 56f., makes a completely incomprehensible remark. In discussing the question whether John was bilingual like others of his Palestinian contemporaries he denies the possibility in connection with John and other analogous cases: 'Josephus, to whom *Schlatter* continually appeals, was not bilingual. He composed the *Jewish Wars* initially in Aramaic [because it was intended for the Jews of the Parthian Diaspora, M.H.]. He had the help of literary Greeks for the Greek version of the *Jewish Wars*, and these Greeks were zealous co-workers in the *Antiquities* as well, as Thackeray... has demonstrated.' The tremendous difference between being bilingual and

having an impeccable literary style is familiar to anyone looking after doctoral students who have to write a dissertation in a language which is not their own. It would be good, given so much lack of thought in other of Haenchen's 'historical-critical' judgments, to be somewhat sceptical here, cf. e.g. my 'Luke the Historian', in *Between Jesus and Paul* (n.8), 199 n.82. In reality Josephus writes a quite orderly *koine* Greek – as in the *Vita*, in *contra Apionem* or in *Antiquities* 20, where he evidently no longer had a ghost writer. The ghost writers did not so much correct the grammar as add the last literary and rhetorical polish. Here, as some rhetorically overloaded parts of the *Antiquities* show, they rather overdid things.

130. Josephus, *Vita* 8-12.

131. Esther 10.31 (LXX); cf. E.Bickerman, 'The Colophon of the Greek Book of Esther', *JBL* 63, 1944, 339-62 with R.Marcus, 'Dositheus. Priest and Levite', *JBL* 64, 1945, 269-71, and P.Kahle, *The Cairo Geniza*, Oxford 1959, 213 n.1. In addition to Hengel, *Judaism and Hellenism* (n.16) I, 64, see now Schürer, *History* III (n.25), 505f., 719-21.

132. Schürer, *History* III (n.25), 474-89; S.Jellicoe, *Studies in the Septuagint: Origins, Recensions and Interpretations. Selected Essays with a Prolegomenon*, LBS, New York 1974.

133. Prologue, v.29; cf. O.Kaiser, 'Judentum und Hellenismus. Ein Beitrag zur Frage nach dem hellenistischen Einfluss auf Kohelet und Jesus Sirach', first published in *VF* 27, 1982, 68-86; in id., *Der Mensch unter dem Schicksal. Studien zur Geschichte, Theologie und Gegenwartsbedeutung der Weisheit*, BZAW 161, Berlin and New York 1985, 135-53, esp.146-8; Schürer, *History* III (n.25), 198-212, and M.Hengel, review of T.Middendorp, *Die Stellung Jesu ben Siras zwischen Judentum und Hellenismus*, Leiden 1973, *JSJ* 5, 1974, 83-7.

134. Hengel, *Judaism and Hellenism* (n.16), I, 97, and H.W.Attridge, 'Historiography', in *Jewish Writings of the Second Temple Period, Apocrypha, Pseudepigrapha, Qumran Sectarian Writings, Philo, Josephus*, ed. M.E.Stone, Compendium Rerum Iudaicarum ad Novum Testamentum 2.3, Assen and Philadelphia 1984, 176-83.

135. Josephus, *Antt.* 20.205, 213.

136. There is a rhetorical analysis of the opening of the speech in S.Lösch, 'Die Dankesrede des Tertullus: Apg 24,1-4', *ThQ* 112, 1931, 295-319.

137. S.Krauss, *Griechische und Lateinische Lehnwörter* (n.28), 2, 301, 343, 377, 630, 643. There is a fine example of an 'orator' (*llwtyyr*) beginning his plea before the king with a *captatio benevolentiae* as in Acts 24.2 in SifDev on Deut.33.2, §343, see M.Hengel, 'Zur matthäischen Bergpredigt und ihrem jüdischen Hintergrund', *ThR* 52, 1987, 327-400: 340.

138. Josephus, *Antt.* 11.317-45; *c.Apionem* 1.192ff. F.Pfister, *Alexander der Grosse in den Offenbarungen der Griechen, Juden, Mohammedaner und Christen*, SSA 3, Berlin 1956; V.Tcherikover, *Hellenistic Civilization and the Jews*, Philadelphia and Jerusalem ²1961, 420 n.17, 431; S.J.D.Cohen, 'Alexander the Great and Jaddua the High Priest according to Josephus', *Association for Jewish Studies Review* 87, 1982/83, 41-68, challenges Alexandrian origins with good reasons.

139. Ps.Hecataeus, in Josephus, *c.Apionem* 1.183b-205a, 213b-214a; 2.43;

Antt. 1.154-168; Clement of Alexandria, *Strom.* 5.113.1-2, German translation by N.Walter, *Fragmente jüdisch-hellenistischer Historiker,* JSHRZ 1.2, *Historische und legendarische Erzählungen,* Gütersloh ²1980, 144-60; cf. Schürer, *History* III (n.25), 671-7.

140. Under Ptolemy IV Philopator (222-205 BCE) he wrote a work about the 'kings of the Jews' the fragments of which are collected in *FGrH* 3 C, no.722; German translation by N.Walter in *Fragmente jüdisch-hellenistischer Exegeten: Aristobul, Demetrius, Aristeas,* JSHRZ 3.2, *Unterweisungen in lehrhaften Form,* Gütersloh 1980, 280-92 (Eusebius, *Praeparatio Evangelica* 9.14.4; 21.1-10; 29.1-3, 15, 16; Clement of Alexandria, *Strom.* 1.141.1-2); cf. Hengel, *Judaism and Hellenism* (n.16) I, 69 and II, 49 n.96; Schürer, *History* III (n.25), 515-17. Here I regard an origin in Alexandria as being more probable.

141. Eusebius, *Praeparatio Evangelica* 9.20.1, 24.1, 37.1-3 (*FGrH* 3 C 273 F 19); German translation by N.Walter in *Fragmente jüdisch-hellenistischer Epik,* JSHRZ 4.3, *Poetische Schriften,* Gütersloh 1983, 135-71; cf. Hengel, *Judaism and Hellenism* (n.16), I, 69 and II, 49 n.97; Schürer, *History* III (n.25), 559-61.

142. Eusebius, *Praeparatio evangelica,* translation by N.Walter, *Fragmente* (n.141). Walter disputes, in my view wrongly, that the author was a Samaritan (ibid., 158f.); Schürer, *History* III (n.25), 561-3: 561, is similarly somewhat sceptical on this matter. The detailed, sympathetic description of the holy or venerable city (the formula ἱερὸν ἄστυ is perhaps used as an analogy for Ἱεροσόλυμα) makes a Jewish origin improbable. The broad account of the conquest of Shechem forms the basis for the later settlement of the 'Israelites' in Shechem. See also M.Hengel, 'Der alte und der neue "Schürer" ', (n.117).

143. Eusebius, *Praeparatio Evangelica* 9.28f.; there is a German translation in E.Vogt, *Tragiker Ezechiel, JSHRZ* 4.3, 112-233; the best edition of the text is now in *Tragicorum Graecorum Fragmenta,* ed. B.Snell, corrected and enlarged edition by R.Kannicht, Göttingen 1986, 288-301, 357: see also Schürer, *History* III (n.25), 563-6, and H.Jacobson, *The Exagoge of Ezekiel.* Cambridge 1983, with D.E.Horst, 'Some Notes on the *Exagoge* of Ezekiel', *Mn* 37, 1984, 354-75.

144. Mendels, *Land of Israel,* (n.117), 109-19, or Walter, JSHRZ 4.3, 142f.

145. E.Bickerman, *The Jews in the Greek Age,* Cambridge, Mass. and London 1988, 233.

146. Ibid.

147. U.Fischer, *Eschatologie und Jenseitserwartung im hellenistischen Diasporajudentum,* BZNW 44, Berlin and New York 1978, 6f.

148. Here Fischer's list tends to confuse the reader. For texts G.Steindorf, *Die Apokalypse des Elias, eine unbekannte Apokalypse und Bruchstücke des Sophonias-Apokalypse, Koptische Texte, Übersetzung, Glossar,* TU 17.3a, Leipzig 1899, and O.S.Wintermute, 'Apocalypse of Zephaniah', in J.H.Charlesworth (ed.), *Old Testament Pseudepigrapha,* Vol.1, Garden City and London 1983, 497-515 (for the basis of the text see 499); id., 'Apocalypse of Isaiah', ibid., 721-53, or A.-M.Denis, PsVTGr 3, Leiden 1977, 129. For the Testament of Abraham see the new edition by F.Schmidt, *Le Testament Grec d'Abraham,* TSAJ 11, Tübingen 1986, or *The Testament of Abraham,* ed. with introduction and notes by

M.R.James, TaS 2.2, Cambridge 1892; also E.Janssen, 'Testament Abrahams', *JSHRZ* 3.2, 193-256; there are introductions and bibliographies in Schürer, *History* III (n.25), 803f., 799-803, 761-7.

149. Fischer, *Eschatologie und Jenseitserwartung* (n.147), 5.

150. Ibid., 6 n.9. For the writings see Schürer, *History* III (n.25), 743-5,757-61,783-6 respectively (for the original language of the *Vitae Prophetarum* see ibid., 705-8, 781-3).

151. Cf. now the rendering by P.Riessler, *Altjüdisches Schrifttum ausserhalb der Bibel*, new edition by H.Getzeny, Freiburg and Heidelberg ⁴1979, 871-80; at the moment the Greek text in the editions by T.Schermann, *Prophetarum vitae fabulosae...*, Leipzig 1907, and C.C.Torrey, *The Lives of the Prophets*, JBL.MS 1, Philadelphia 1946, should still be used. One might suppose that the whole collection of lives, a kind of lexicon of the prophets with numerous hagiographical and geographical details, could also have been used by Jewish pilgrims from the Diaspora as a geographical travel guide indicating the places where the tombs of the prophets were located. I owe this comment to my assistant, Frau A.M.Schwemer, who is working on a translation of and commentary on the *Vitae* for JSHRZ; she conjectures that the original language was Greek.

152. H.W.Hollander and M.de Jonge, *The Testaments of the Twelve Patriarchs. A Commentary*, SVTP 8, Leiden 1985, 130 (TestLevi); 185 (the author of TestJos knows the geography of Palestine). For the Phaedra motive see M.Braun, *History and Romance in Graeco-Oriental Literature*, Oxford 1983, 44-93, and my *Judaism and Hellenism* (n.16) I, 111.

153. Schürer, *History* III (n.25), 767-81.

154. The part played by Alexandria is still the most significant here; it breaks off completely with the catastrophe of the rebellion under Trajan in 115-117 CE (Schürer I [n.25], 389-94, 398; III, 92-4, 127-9). The Alexandrian heritage was taken over by the Christians.

155. Josephus, *Antt.*, 14.215; for synagogues in Rome in the time of Augustus see *CIJ* 284, 365; for the reign of Tiberius, Josephus, *Antt.* 18.81-84; cf. also *CIJ* 301, 416, 425, 496 or *CIJ* 1-514. For the origin of the community see Philo, *Leg.Gai.* 154-8; Suetonius, *Tiberius*, 36.

156. M.Hengel, 'Anonymität, Pseudepigraphie und "Literarische Fälschung" in der jüdisch-hellenistischen Literatur', in *Pseudepigraphie I, Entretiens sur l'Antiquité Classique* 18, Vandoeuvres-Geneva 1971/72, 229-329.

157. H.Gressmann, 'Die Aufgaben der Wissenschaft des nachbiblischen Judentums', ZAW NF.1 (= 43), 1925, 1-32, here esp.3-5; K.Berger in his earlier publications, but cf. also his extremely unclear and indeed misleading challenge to this (in id., *Hermeneutik des Neuen Testaments*, Gütersloh 1988, 48). Berger claims that 'the New Testament authors frequently take the concrete content of their norms from outside (from the sphere of *Hellenistic Judaism* [my italics], apocalyptic or pagan Hellenism); similarly also G.Strecker, *The Sermon on the Mount. An Exegetical Commentary*, Edinburgh and Nashville 1988 (on this see my 'Zur matthäischen Bergpredigt' [n.137], 327-400).

158. For detailed information about literature and text see above, 51f. n.93 pp.93f. and nn.270-82.

159. See above, pp.47f. and below, pp.91f. nn.249-55.

160. Cf. M.Hengel, 'Die Arbeit im frühen Christentum', *ThBeitr* 17, 1986, 174-212, here esp.176ff., 184f.

161. M.Hengel, *Nachfolge und Charisma. Eine exegetisch-religionsgeschichtliche Studie zu Mt. 8.21f. und Jesu Ruf in die Nachfolge*, BZNW 34, Berlin 1968, 34 (also 15 n.41); cf. bYom 35b Bar and bSot 21a.

162. SifBam on Num.18.20, §119; for the Pharisees see also Jeremias, *Jerusalem* (n.46), 246-67.

163. Cf. the following sayings attributed to Hillel in the Mishnah: MAb 1.13, 'He that learns not is worthy of death' (this rhymes in the Aramaic); ibid., 2.5: 'A brutish man dreads not sin, and an ignorant man cannot be saintly' (in H.Danby [ed.], *The Mishnah*, Oxford 1930, 447, 448). Even if it was to be carried out for its own sake and not for other purposes, the study of the Torah was a decisive prerequisite of social ascent or of acquiring greater social prestige (Matt.23.6f.). The Christian polemic in Matt.23, which in itself is unjust, is to be understood against this background.

164. S.Applebaum, 'Jewish Urban Communities and Greek Influences', *Scripta Classical Israelica* 6, 1979/80, 158-75; G.M.Cohen, 'The Hellenistic Military Colony: A Herodian Example', *TPAPA* 103, 1972, 83-95.

165. Y.Meshorer, *Jewish Coins* (n.27), Plates II/III, nos.5, 5a, 7, 8, 9: 'ΒΑΣΙΛΕΩΣ ΑΛΕΞΑΝΔΡΟΥ' (n.27), see above, p.8; cf. Schürer, *History* I (n.25), 219-28, 603f.; cf. also Hengel, 'Rabbinische Legende' (n.110), 36-41.

166. J.Jeremias, *Heiligengräber in Jesu Umwelt (Mt.23.29; Lk.11.47). Eine Untersuchung zur Volksreligion der Zeit Jesu*, Göttingen 1958, 50.

167. I Macc.13.25-30: for the location see Jeremias, *Heiligengräber* (n.166), 50 and n.9.

168. Jeremias, *Heiligengräber* (n.166), 50.

169. G.O.Neuhaus, *Studien zu den poetischen Stücken im 1.Makkabäerbuch*, fzB 12, Würzburg 1974, 144-53.

170. Cf. already I Macc.2.46; 13.13-48; also Josephus, *Antt.* 13.257, 318f., 397 and Hengel, *Zealots* (n.48), 197-200.

171. See P.Vidal-Naquet, *Flavius Josèphe ou du bon usage de la tradition*, Paris 1977, 43; E.Will and C.Orrieux, *Ioudaismos-Hellénismos. Essai sur le Judaisme Judéen à l'époque hellénistique*, Nancy 1986, 190-3.

172. Cf.Strabo, 16.2.28 (*GLAJ* Vol.1, no.114, pp.290-4 with commentary); Josephus, *Antt.* 14.28; Diodore 40.2 (*GLAJ*, Vol.1, no.64, pp.185-7) for the alleged attacks on the Romans.

173. L.Y.Rahmani, 'Jason's Tomb', *IEJ* 17, 1967, 61-100 and P.Benoit, 'L'inscription grecque du tombeau de Jason', *IEJ* 17, 1967, 112f.

174. Bickerman, *The Jews in the Greek Age* (n.145), 231.

175. 'Epicureans', cf. mSanh 10.1 (cf. the explanations in H.Danby [ed.], *The Mishnah* [n.163]), mAb 2.14.

176. Alongside Josephus, *Antt.* 18.376, see bQid 66b. For the word see also

jSanh 9.27d; bSanh99b; brHSh 17a and bHag 5b. For the person see also Hengel, 'Rabbinische Legende' (n.110), see above p.8.

177. bBQ 82b; cf. S.Lieberman, *Hellenism in Jewish Palestine. Studies in the I Century BCE – IV Century CE*, TSJTSA 18, New York ²1962, 100-14.

178. Cf. the correspondence between Libanius of Antioch and the Jewish patriarch (and the introduction by M.Stern in *GLAJ*, Vol. 2, pp.580-3), whose son studied with Libanius (Ep.1098.1-2 or *GLAJ*, Vol.2, no.502, pp.595f.): a translation is most easily accessible in *GLAJ*, Vol.2, nos.496-503, pp.589-99.

179. Schalit, *König Herodes* (n.56), index 803, s.v. 'Hellenismus im Staate des Herodes (Heerwesen, Verwaltung, Rechtsprechung, Hofleben, Baukunst und Herrscherkult'); G.Prause, *Herodes der Grosse. König der Juden*, Hamburg 1971 (which is too one-sided); H.Merkel, 'Herodes der Grosse', *RAC* 14, 833, refers to the statues of Herod in the Greek cities; cf. Josephus, *Antt.* 14.153 and Schürer, *History* II (n.25), 52 n.143.

180. See G.Hölscher, 'Josephus.2', *PRE* 9, Stuttgart 1916, 1934-2000, here 1944f.; Jacoby, *FGrH* 2C, commentary 229-291: 230; cf. W.Otto, 'Herodes.14', *PRE* Supplement 2, 1-200, here esp.26ff. and the additions in 9, 2513. But I think that Nicolaus was used directly, see also B.Z.Wacholder, *Nicolaus of Damascus*, UCPH 75, Berkeley 1962; Schürer, *History* I (n.25), 26f., 28-32, with Hengel, *Zealots* (n.48) 8 and n.14; for the problem of sources in Josephus cf. also L.H.Feldman, *Josephus and Modern Scholarship (1937-1980)*, Berlin and New York 1984, 402-6 (18: Josephus Sources, 18.2: Nicolaus of Damascus).

181. The most accessible source of information about the enormous extent of his palace in Hellenistic-Roman Jericho (Tulul Abu'l-Alajik) on both sides of the Wadi el-Qelt is O.Keel and M.Küchler, *Orte und Landschaften der Bibel. Ein Handbuch und Studienreiseführer zum Heiligen Land*, 2, *Der Süden*, Zurich etc. 1982, 500-12. Mention should also be made here of the further Herodian fortresses of Cyprus (Tell el-Aqabe, see Keel/Küchler, 513-16); Alexandreion (Qarn Sartabe, Keel/Küchler, 563-7), the Hasmonaean fortress rebuilt by Herod (*BJ* 1, 308); and the fortress of Hyrcania, which can still largely be seen today (Strabo 16.2.40 = *GLAJ*, Vol. 1, no.115, pp.297, 302; Keel/Küchler, 587-93); also the fortress of Machaerus with the baths of Callirhoe on the east shore of the Dead Sea which Pliny mentions in his *Natural History* (5.72 = *GLAJ*, Vol. 1, no.204, pp.469, 471f.); cf. Keel/Küchler, 447-50. In Callirhoe an attempt was made on Herod's life by the bathing attendants (Josephus, *BJ*, 1.657f.).

182. Y.Yadin, *Masada*, London and New York 1966, 4-54 (the northern palace-villa), 58-73 (middle and upper terraces), 75-85 (baths), 117-132 (western palace). Although the assimilation to contemporary Roman provincial architecture is great, it is 'interesting that Herod, even in his buildings at Masada, was reluctant to offend the susceptibilities of his family and Jewish citizens, and he did not therefore resort to representations of the human form and of animals in his mosaics'(ibid., 119) but only geometrical motifs and leaf-patterns (illustrations ibid., 124f.). There is some dispute as to whether a synagogue also belonged to the period of Hellenistic building (thus ibid., 185); for this see most recently L.L.Grabbe, 'Synagogues in pre-70 Palestine:

A Reassessment', *JTS* 39, 1988, 401-10, esp.406, and E.Netzer, 'The Synagogues in Massada, Herodium, Gamla and Magdala (?) from the Architect's Viewpoint', in *Synagogues in Antiquity* (n.43).

183. E.Netzer's monograph (*Greater Herodium*, Qedem 13, Jerusalem 1981) is to be supplemented by some new discoveries, see E.Netzer and S.Arzi, 'The Tunnels of Herodium', *Qadmoniot* 69/70, 1985, 33-8 (in Hebrew) or Netzer's guide (*Herodium. An Archaeological Guide*, Jerusalem 1987). The tomb of the king mentioned in *BJ* 1, 670-3, has not so far been discovered (cf. *BJ* 1, 418-21). It has been conjectured that Herodium was modelled on the Mausoleum of Augustus which was erected in Rome in 28 BCE (thus A.Segal, 'Herodium', *IEJ* 23, 1973, 27-9). However, that can hardly be right, for two reasons. It is still unclear *where* the tomb of Herod was (see above). Moreover, there is almost no similarity between the mausoleum of Augustus, which had a drum shape rising from a rectangular pedestal, and Herodium, a fortress which consisted of a round building framed by four towers (thus also Netzer, *Guide*, 28); alongside the mountain fortress, which had a triclinium and a Roman bath with hypocaust heating, an extensive complex of 15 hectares, 'Lower Herodium', has been discovered which similarly had baths, a kind of hippodrome (as its function is so far unclear the excavators have called it 'the course', cf. Netzer, *Guide*, 37), and a palace building. A 'monumental building' can be interpreted as the triclinium of a tomb building and thus would form an analogy to buildings in Petra (Netzer, *Guide*, 39). Netzer wonders whether spoils in the Byzantine 'central church' come from the opening up of Herod's tomb (ibid., 40). Herodian cisterns have also been recently discovered: E.Netzer, 'Jewish Rebels Dig Strategic Tunnel', *BAR* 15, 1988, 18-33.

184. There is a bibliography and a description of the complex of buildings in Keel/Küchler (n.181), 670-96.

185. Ibid., 696-713.

186. For Antipatris see M.Hengel, 'Luke the Historian', in *Between Jesus and Paul* (n.8), 119f.: Herod settled in Antipatris Samaritans and Jews who were driven out on the founding of Sebaste (Syncellus 584, ed. A.A.Mosshammer 373.5); for Phasaelis see Keel/Küchler (n.181), 562f. and the bibliography there.

187. For the name see Schürer, *History* II (n.25), 116 with nn.163f.

188. So far there is only literary evidence for this building; cf. Josephus, *Antt.* 17.255 and *BJ* 2.44, with Schalit, *König Herodes* (n.56), 403. Jeremias, *Jerusalem* (n.46), 10, makes a suggestion about the possible location of the Jerusalem hippodrome; for the amphitheatre see *BJ* 1.667. M.Lämmer has made several studies of the use of such Herodian buildings: 'Griechische Wettkämpfe in Jerusalem und ihre politischen Hintergründe', *Kölner Beiträge zur Sportwissenschaft* 2, Schorndorf 1974, 182-227 (on *Antt.* 16, 267-79 and the course of the festival of the Pentaeteris with games in honour of the Emperor); id., 'Die Kaiserspiele von Caesarea im Dienste der Politik des Königs Herodes', *Kölner Beiträge zur Sportwissenschaft* 3, Schorndorf 1975, 95-164 (on *Antt.*16.136-41 and *BJ* 1.415); id., 'Eine Propaganda-Aktion des Königs Herodes in Olympia', *Perspektiven der Sportwissenschaft*, Schorndorf 1973, 160-

73 (on *Antt.* 16.149/*BJ* 1.426f.). For the Jericho theatre, in addition to *Antt.*17.194 see also Keel/Küchler (n.181), 501, 512; the tomb of the Goliath family was west of the hippodrome (above, p.11 n.41).

189. J.L.Kelso and D.C.Baramki, 'Excavations at New Testament Jericho and Khirbet En-Nitla...', *AASOR* 29/30, 1949/51, 10 (cited in Schalit, *König Herodes* [n.56], 402f. n.882).

190. Hengel, 'Qumran und der Hellenismus' (n.100), 333-72; A.Strobel, 'Die Wasseranlagen von Hirbet Qumran', *ZDPV* 88, 1972, 55-86; cf. the water system on the temple mount: Ben-Dov, *In the Shadow of the Temple* (n.53), 117-19.

191. Schürer, *History* II (n.25), 312, 317; cf. the index under Herod (ibid., III, 940f.).

192. Ibid. I, 445-7, 451; II, 82, 117. See the coin on the cover.

193. It is difficult to know how to estimate two representations of Roman deities in this connection in Jerusalem: a gem which depicts Hermes (Avigad, 'Excavations' [n.47], 49) and the impression of a seal of Zeus the Thunderer (R.Amiran and A.Eitan, 'Excavations in the Jerusalem Citadel', ibid., 54); these have not yet been dated clearly, nor have they been published in a form from which conclusions may be drawn. In mZab 1.5 a *gd ywn* appears as the designation of a place; this is probably to be understood as the statue of a Greek god of good fortune, perhaps the Tyche of the city which is so frequent in Hellenistic cities in the neighbourhood of Siloah (cf. bSan 63b). 'In Semitic Τύχη as a god's name is rendered *gad*' (Schürer, *Geschichte* 2 [n.73], 34 n.60). This place designation may be a reminiscence of the pagan military colony on the Acra (167-141 BCE) or may come from the period after 70. The same goes for the archaeological discoveries mentioned; cf. also my *Judaism and Hellenism* (n.16), I, 158f., for the Ptolemaean period. The protest against the golden eagle which Herod had put on the temple shows how sensitive people were in Jerusalem over the question of idols (see below, n.204). The discovery of fragments of a relief aedicula and other dedicatory reliefs in the excavations of the pool of Bethesda has already been known for some time (see e.g. C.Watzinger, *Denkmäler Palästinas. Eine Einführung in die Archäologie des Heiligen Landes* 2, Leipzig 1935, 85f. plate 7). A.Duprez, *Jésus et les dieux guérisseurs, à propos de Jean V*, CRB 12, Paris 1970, has associated these discoveries, which indicate an Asclepius-Serapis cult in Aelia, with John 5, and interpreted the passage as a 'polemical text' against this cult. But that is extremely improbable.

194. Schalit, *König Herodes* (n.56), 329.

195. Josephus, *Antt.* 15.383, 387 (LCL, Josephus 8, 187).

196. Schürer, *History* I (n.25), 373, is a guide to the discovery of these inscriptions, which are attested by Josephus (*BJ* 6.125). The text is in Dittenberger, *OGIS* 598 or *CIJ* 1400; there is a second version in *SEG* 8, 109. Further bibliography and the text in Schürer, *History* III (n.25), 285f. n.57; special mention should be made of E.Bickerman, 'The Warning Inscription of Herod's Temple', first in *JQR* 37, 1946/47, 387-405, now in id., *Studies in Jewish and Christian History* 2, AGJU 9.2, Leiden 1980, 210-24.

197. On this cf. p.33 and 83 n.180 and Schürer, *History* I (n.25), 28-32 (editions of the text and bibliography, 31f.), also Hengel, *Judaism and Hellenism* (n.16) I, 77; R.Laqueur, 'Nikolaos 20', *PRE* 17.1, Stuttgart 1936, 362-424; Millar, 'The Problem of Hellenistic Syria' (n.3), 125; B.Z.Wacholder, *Nicolaus of Damascus*, UCPH, Berkeley and Los Angeles 1962.

198. For Damascus see A.Barrois, 'Damascus', *DBS* 2, Paris 1934, 275-87; E.Cavaignac, 'Damas de 125-29 av.J.C.', in *Mélanges bibliques A.Robert*, Paris 1957, 348-53. We do not know when the city attained the status of a Greek *polis*. Perhaps this happened through Antiochus IV.

199. Josephus, *Antt.* 1, 159f.; Eusebius, *Praeparatio Evangelica* 9.16 (= *GLAJ*, Vol.1, no.83, pp.233f.); cf. Pompeius Trogus in Justin, *Hist.Phil.*, *Lib.36 Epitoma*, 2.1 (= *GLAJ* 1, no.137, pp.335, 337 with commentary, 339). See also J.S.Siker, 'Abraham in Graeco-Roman Paganism', *JSJ* 18, 1987, 177-208: 192f.

200. The evidence in the text, which has been preserved by Constantine VII Porphyrogenitus (912-952) (*Excerpta de virtutibus* I, in Büttner-Wobst, 327) is most easily accessible in *GLAJ*, Vol.1, no.96, 248-50; cf. ibid., no.94, p.246.

201. 'The composition of the historical works under Herod's auspices presupposes a fairly large Greek library in Jerusalem' (Wacholder, *Nicolaus* [n.197], 48; appendix 'Greek Authors in Herod's Library', 81-6; cf. also Schalit, *König Herodes* [n.56], 412f. n.932).

202. Ibid.

203. See the intervention by Nicolaus of Damascus before Marcus Agrippa for the Ionian cities on behalf of the king (Josephus, *Antt.* 16.27-65); cf. also *Antt.*16.299,333 with *GLAJ* 1, no.95, pp.246-8 (see above, pp.9ff.). For mentions of Herod in ancient Greek and Latin authors see Stern, *GLAJ* 3, 125, index: Persius, *Sat.* 5.180, calls the sabbath *Herodis... dies*, ibid. 1, 436; cf. also Augustus' pun on Herod's pig and son, Macrobius, *Sat.* 2.4.11, ibid., 2.665. For Ptolemaeus (of Ashkelon?), see ibid. 1, 355f.

204. Josephus, *BJ* 1.648-50; cf. excursus III, 'Der Adler am Tempel zu Jerusalem' in the Greek/German edition of *De Bello Judaico* edited by O.Michel and O.Bauernfeind, Darmstadt 1959, 425; Hengel, *Zealots* (n.48), 332f.

205. Hengel, *Zealots* (n.48), 328; for slaves see Jeremias, *Jerusalem* (n.46), 312-17 or 345-51.

206. L.Baeck, *Paulus, die Pharisäer und das Neue Testament*, Frankfurt 1961, 87 (= *Die Pharisäer. Ein Kapitel jüdischer Geschichte*, Berlin 1934, 89).

207. Schürer, *History* II (n.25), 363-9; N.N.Glatzer, *Repräsentant des klassischen Judentums*, Bibliotheka Judaica, Frankfurt am Main 1966, 19; cf. similarly E.E.Urbach, *The Sages. Their Concepts and Beliefs*, Vol.1, Jerusalem 1979, 576-93; there is a critical analysis in J.Neusner, *The Rabbinic Traditions about the Pharisees before 70. Part 1. The Masters*, Leiden 1971, 212-302; for Hillel and the Jerusalem of Herod see still Wachholder, *Nicolaus* (n.197), 44-9, and his interesting comparison between the maxims of Hillel and texts of Nicolaus.

There is now dispute over whether the patriarchs are descended from

Hillel, since there is little evidence for this. However, there is no doubt that R.Gamaliel II, the first patriarch, consistently developed Hillel's *tendencies*.

208. Sepphoris: Schürer, *History* II (n.25), 172-6; Julias: ibid., 176-8 (cf.also I, 342); for the location cf. ibid., 178; cf. also S.J.D.Cohen, *Josephus in Galilee and Rome. His* Vita *and Development as a Historian*, Columbia Studies in the Classical Tradition 8, Leiden 1979, 244-6; S.Freyne, *Galilee from Alexander the Great to Hadrian* (n.70), 122f.; id., *Galilee, Jesus and the Gospels* (n.70), 137-43, 144-66, 170-3; Y.Meshorer, 'Sepphoris and Rome', in *Greek Numismatics and Archaeology. Essays in Honor of M.Thompson*, Brussels 1979, 159-71; S.S.Miller, *Studies in the History and Traditions of Sepphoris*, SJLA 37, Leiden 1984; S.Seyrig, 'Eirenopolis-Neronias-Sepphoris', *NumC* 10, 1950, 284-9; for Hadrian's policy see my 'Hadrians Politik gegenüber Juden und Christen', in *Ancient Studies in Memory of Elias Bikerman, JANES* 16-17, 1984-85, 153-82.

209. M.Avi-Jona, 'The Foundation of Tiberias', *IEJ* 1, 1950/51, 160-9; cf. also Josephus: according to *Antt.* 18.36-38 a motley (σύγκλυδες) public was settled in the city which consisted both of a proletariat without possessions and to some degree also without freedom, and members of the better classes; until the second century the rabbis regarded the city as unclean. Cf. also Schürer,*History* II (n.25), 178-82 (also I, 342) and Freyne, *Galilee, Jesus and the Gospels* (n.70), 137-40; cf. also index s.v.

210. Josephus, *Vita*, 65-7; Schürer, *History* II (n.25), 178-83; G.Foerster, 'The Excavations of Tiberias', *Qad.* 10, 1977, 87-91 (in Hebrew).

211. tSukk 4.6 (Lieberman 273); jSukk 5.1 (Krotoschin 55a line 72 – 55b line 8) and bSukk 51b. Compare my 'Proseuche und Synagoge. Jüdische Gemeinde, Gotteshaus und Gottesdienst in der Diaspora und in Palästina', in *Tradition und Glaube. Das frühe Christentum in seiner Umwelt. Festgabe für K.G.Kuhn*, ed. G.Jeremias, H.-W.Kuhn and H.Stegemann, Göttingen 1971, 157-84: 168 n.44.

212. A.Kasher, 'Synagogues in Ptolemaic and Roman Egypt as Community Centers', in *Synagogues in Antiquity* (n.43), and H.-P.Stähli, *Antike Synagogenkunst*, Stuttgart 1988, 18f. (parts are very superficial).

213. Schürer, *History* II (n.25), 181; Josephus, *BJ* 2.599; 3.453. According to *Vita* 58, the function of the archon Jesus son of Sapphias consisted in presiding over the *boule* with 600 members (*BJ* 2.615). Josephus also mentions in *Vita* 13 the council of the δέκα πρῶτοι, hyparchs (*BJ* 2.615) and the *agoranomos* (*Antt.* 18.149, see Schürer, *History* II [n.25], 180 n.520); for the designation of the citizens see ibid., 180, nn.514, 523.

214. M.Lämmer, *Griechische Wettkämpfe in Galiläa unter der Herrschaft des Herodes Antipas*, Kölner Beiträge zur Sportwissenschaft 5, Schorndorf 1977, 37-67, conjectures that 'athletic, equestrian and musical events must have taken place there' (52). In Lämmer's view the games were held in honour of the emperor, as cultic honours for Antipas were not possible.

215. According to Josephus, *Antt.* 18.149, for a short time Agrippa I was *agoranomos* of Tiberias; for his pious attitude see Schürer, *History* I (n.25), 443-54 and II, 117 n.168; for Agrippa's titles, ibid. I, 451f.; for the death of Agrippa, *Antt.* 19.343-52 and Acts 12.21-23; Schürer, *History* I, 452f. with

nn.43f. According to both reports the king died after being hailed as god by the pagan population of Caesarea; for comparable texts from the context see Conzelmann, *Acts* (n.61), 96f. The pagan mobs in Caesarea and Sebaste erupted for joy at the death of the king.

216. Hengel, *Zealots* (n.48), 313-76.

217. Josephus, *Antt.* 20.173-8, 182-4; *BJ* 2.266-70, 284; for the dating of Nero's rescript see Schürer, *History* II (n.25), 117 n.168.

218. Josephus, *BJ* 2.309 (cf. M.Hengel, *Crucifixion*, London and Philadelphia 1977, 39-45:40); for Gessius Florus see *Antt.* 20.252f.; *BJ* 2.277-9 with Schürer, *History* I [n.25], 470, 485-6).

219. Cf. M.Goodman, 'The First Jewish Revolt: Social Conflict and the Problem of Debt', *JJS* 33, 1982, 417-26; id., *The Ruling Class of Judaea. The Origins of Jewish Revolt against Rome AD 66-70*, Cambridge 1987, with the review by E.Bammel, *JTS* 40, 1989, 378-85.

220. G.Theissen, 'Das "schwankende Rohr" (Mt.11,7) und die Gründungs-münzen von Tiberias', *ZDPV* 101, 1985, 43-55. Theissen had developed his programme of research under the title 'Lokalkoloritforschung in den Evangelien. Plädoyer für die Erneuerung einer alten Fragestellung', *EvTh* 45, 1985, 481-500 ('Research into Local Colouring in the Gospels – A Plea for the Revival of an Old Question'). His articles are now collected in *Lokalkolorit und Zeitgeschichte in den Evangelien. Ein Beitrag zur Geschichte der synoptischen Tradition*, NTOA 8, Fribourg CH and Göttingen 1989.

221. W.F.Arndt, F.W.Gingrich and W.Bauer, *A Lexicon of New Testament Greek*, Chicago ²1979, 303. See above, pp.17f.

222. A.Alt, 'Die Stätten des Wirkens Jesu' (n.90). However, in my view some corrections are necessary to Alt's picture of a strict division between Jewish and Hellenistic settlements, like Nazareth and Sepphoris, as I have demonstrated above; see now also Freyne, *Galilee, Jesus and the Gospels* (n.70), 139f.

223. John 6.1,23; 21.1; for the social background see my *The Johannine Question*, London and Philadelphia 1989.

224. Hengel, 'Luke the Historian', in *Between Jesus and Paul* (n.8), 193 n.19; Lang, 'Über Tyros und Sidon' (n.48).

225. E.Plümacher, *Identitätsverlust und Identitätsgewinn: Studien zum Verhältnis von kaiserzeitlicher Stadt und frühem Christentum*, BTS 11, Neukirchen-Vluyn 1987.

226. H.Merklein, 'Die Ekklesia Gottes. Der Kirchenbegriff bei Paulus und in Jerusalem', first published in *BZ* NF 23, 1979, 48-70; in id., *Studien zu Jesus und Paulus*, WUNT 43, Tübingen 1987, 296-318, esp. 303-5 with n.51.

227. See my 'Between Jesus and Paul' and 'Christology and New Testament Chronology', both in *Between Jesus and Paul* (n.8).

228. See my *Nachfolge und Charisma* (n.161), 31-3 ('Here [Epictetus, *Diss.* 3.22, 45-49] we certainly have the closest philosophical analogy to the sayings about discipleship in Q, Matt.8.18-22 and Luke 9.57-62' [33]), 35,37; for the problem see C.Schneider, *Geistesgeschichte des Christentums* 1, Munich 1954, 29-99; E.Wechssler, *Hellas im Evangelium*, Hamburg 1936. See also F.G.Downing,

'Cynics and Christians', *NTS* 30, 1984, 584-93; id., 'The Social Contexts of Jesus the Teacher', *NTS* 33, 1987, 439-51; id., *Jesus and the Threat of Freedom*, London 1987; id., *Christ and the Cynics*, JSOT.MS 4, Sheffield 1988.

229. In particular the third Sibylline, with its various strata from the second and first centuries BCE, and the fifth Sibylline (second century CE) belong to Egypt; the fourth may have been composed in Rome around 80 CE; see H.Lichtenberger, 'Täufergemeinden und frühchristliche Täuferpolemik im letzten Drittel des 1.Jahrhunderts', *ZTK* 84, 1987, 36-57 (38-43) and Millar, 'Empire, Community and Culture' (n.3), 158f.

230. For the understanding of the earliest Christian message of the atoning death of Jesus see my *The Atonement* (n.6), also in *The Cross of the Son of God* (n.6), 189-292. There is also a wealth of material in M.Hadas, *Hellenistic Culture. Fusion and Diffusion*, New York and London 1959; E.J.Bickerman, *The Jews in the Greek Age* (n.145: above all in Part 3, 'Permanence and Innovation', 133-305); numerous lesser investigations by M.Philonenko are also important: 'David et Orphée', *RHPR* 47, 1967, 353-7; 'La cosmologie du Livre des Secrets d'Henoch', in *Religions en Égypte hellénistique et romaine*, Paris 1969, 109-16; 'Juda et Héraklès', *RHPR* 50, 1970, 60-2; 'Iphigénie et Sheila', in *Les syncrétismes dans les religions grecque et romaine*, Paris 1973, 270-9; 'Un mystère juif', in *Mystères et syncrétiennes*, Paris 1975, 65-70; 'La sixième vision de IV Esdras et les "Oracles d'Hystaspè"', in F.Raphael (et al.), *L'Apocalyptique*, Études d'Histoire des Religions 3, Paris 1977, 129-35; 'Paradoxes stoiciens dans le Testament de Lévi', in *Sagesse et Religion. Bibliothèque des centres d'études supérieures spécialisés, Colloque du Strasbourg, Octobre 1976*, Paris 1979, 99-104; 'Deux horoscopes qumrâniens: Identifications des personnages', *RHPR* 65, 1985, 61-6.

231. Hengel, *Judaism and Hellenism* I (n.16), III.6, 'The Hasidim and the First Climax of Jewish Apocalyptic' (175-217), and my 'Anonymität, Pseudepigraphie und literarische Fälschung' (n.156); also 'Messianische Hoffnung und politischer "Radikalismus" in der "jüdisch-hellenistischen Diaspora"', in *Apocalypticism*, ed. D.Hellholm, Tübingen [2]1989, 655-86.

232. Dan.2.1-49 with Hesiod, *Works and Days* 1.109-201:156-73; cf. my *Judaism and Hellenism* I, 182-4 with notes; D.Flusser, 'The Four Empires in the Fourth Sibyl and in the Book of Daniel', *Israel Oriental Studies* 2, 1972, 148-75; D.Mendels, 'The Five Empires. A note on a Propagandistic Topos', *AJP* 102, 1981, 330-7.

233. L.Baeck, *Paulus, die Pharisäer und das Neue Testament* (n.206), Frankfurt 1961, 15, made the amazing judgment: 'The book of Daniel was written when for a century Palestine had been part of the Ptolemaic empire... and was under the cultural influence of its Hellenism... We do not know whether the new concept of messiah which appears in the book of Daniel derives from Palestine or from Egypt. At all events this new form of the messianic idea fits the basic idea of the Alexandrian philologists amazingly well. The messianism of the lofty had found an ally but at the same time this could have been a loftier seducer'. R.Kearns, *Das Traditionsgefügen üm den Menschensohn*, Tübingen 1986,

argues for Egyptian influence from the Ptolemaic period on the conception of the Son of Man.

234. Cf. e.g. SyrBar 30.1-5; 49.1-52.7; (Strack) Billerbeck IV, 1166-98: 1175f.

235. Josephus, *BJ* 2.154, 'τὰς δὲ ψυχὰς ἀθανάτους ἀεὶ διαμένειν'; cf. H.Lichtenberger, *Studien zum Menschenbild in Texten der Qumrangemeinde*, SUNT 15, Göttingen 1980, 218-31. I hear from a reliable source that for almost thirty years the existence has been known of a major fragment from 4Q which shows that the Essenes taught the physical resurrection. However, like many other fragments, it has been withheld from publication by the authorities. See now the Ezekiel Apocryphon, ed. J.Strugnell and D.Dimant, '4Q Second Ezekiel (4Q 385)', in *Mémorial J.Carmignac*, ed. F.García Martínez and É.Puech, *Revue de Qumran* 13, 1988, 45-58.

236. The types produced by N.Walter, '"Hellenistische Eschatologie" im Frühjudentum - Ein Beitrag zur "Biblischen Theologie"?', *TLZ* 110, 1985, 331-48, are therefore all problematical. The contrasts that he works out tend to flow together much more strongly than is evident in his account (ibid., 335).

237. H.C.C.Cavallin, *Life after Death. Paul's Argument for the Resurrection of the Dead in I Cor.15. Part I, An Enquiry into the Jewish Background*, CB.NT 7.1, Lund 1974, collects all the material together. Ps.Phocylides 102-104, 115, where resurrection faith and the immortality of the soul are postulated side by side, is typical.

238. EthEn 22.1-14; Hengel, *Judaism and Hellenism* (n.16) I, 197f. with nn.582-7; ibid., 188f.

239. M.Nilsson, *Geschichte der Griechischen Religion*, HAW 5.2, Vol.1, *Die Religion Griechenlands bis auf die griechische Weltherrschaft*, reprint of ³1967, Munich 1976, 332ff., 615ff., 620ff.; Vol.2, *Die hellenistische und römische Zeit*, Munich ³1974, 1556ff.; W.Burkert, *Griechische Religion der archaischen und klassischen Epoche*, 1977, 201ff., 301-6, 436ff.; id., *Die orientalisierende Epoche in der griechischen Religion und Literatur*, SHAW.PH 1, 1984, Heidelberg 1984.

240. In addition to Pytheas of Massalia, who reports the great sea-voyage which he really undertook (F.Lasserre, 'Pytheas 4', *KP* 4, Munich 1979, 1272-4), mention should be made e.g. of Euhemerus, who at the end of the fourth century/beginning of the third century BCE composed a travel romance ἱερὰ ἀναγραφή (cf. K.Thraede, 'Euhemerismus', *RAC* 6, Stuttgart 1966, 877-90) and Iamblichus, the second-century CE author of romances, who came from Syria (W.Röllig, 'Jamblichos 3', *KP* 2, Munich 1979, 1307); for the subject see also N.Holzberg, *Der antike Roman. Eine Einführung*, Artemis Einführungen 25, Munich and Zurich 1986.

241. Test Lev 2.7-10; 3.1-10; cf. W.Bousset, *Die Himmelsreise der Seele*, ARW 4, 1901, 136-69, 229-73, reissued Darmstadt 1960; J.S.D.Tabor, *Things Unutterable. Paul's Ascent to Paradise and its Greco-Roman, Judaic and Early Christian Contexts*, New York and London 1986.

242. Hengel, *Judaism and Hellenism* (n.16), 204f. with bibliography in n.622.

243. Typical of this is e.g. the verdict of W.Schneemelcher, *Das Urchristentum*, 101 (on Acts 6.1): 'There (viz. in 'primitive Palestinian Christianity', M.H.)

will at a very early stage have been a Hellenistic Jewish Christianity alongside the Jewish Christians who largely spoke Aramaic and were dominated by apocalyptic' – as if the latter were less 'dominated by apocalyptic'!

244. The dawn of the 'new aeon' begins from the heavenly world: the stone which destroys the four world empires falls from above, from the mountain (of God) (Dan.2.45; in v.34 'mountain' should be added); the Son of Man comes (Dan.7.13) 'on the clouds *of heaven*', and from there also comes Michael, the 'support' for Israel (Dan.12.1). The whole Apocalypse of John is permeated with the certainty that redemption comes from heaven, cf. Rev.4.5; 21.1ff.

245. G.W.E.Nickelsburg Jr, 'Apocalyptic and Myth in I Enoch 6-11', *JBL* 96, 1977, 383-405, esp.395-7, 399-404.

246. P.D.Hanson, 'Rebellion in Heaven, Azazel, and Euhemeristic Heroes in I Enoch 6-11', *JBL* 96, 1977, 195-233.

247. K.Thraede, 'Erfinder II (geistesgeschichtlich)', *RAC* 5, Stuttgart 1982, 1191-1278: 1241-5, and Hengel, *Judaism and Hellenism* I (n.16), 89f., 266.

248. J.Maier, 'Geister (Dämonen) B.I 1.c.Israel', *RAC* 9, Stuttgart 1976, 579-85, and id., 'Geister (Dämonen) B.III, Frühes und hellenistisches Judentum', 626-40; E.Schweizer, 'Geister (Dämonen) C.I. Neues Testament', 688-700, with bibliography at the end; F.Andres, *Die Engellehre der griechischen Apologeten des zweiten Jahrhunderts und ihr Verhältnis zur griechisch-römischen Dämonologie*, FChLDG 12/3, Paderborn 1914.

249. See my 'Qumran und der Hellenismus' (n.100).

250. J.Duhaime, 'The *War Scroll* from Qumran and the Greco-Roman Tactical Treatises', *RdQ* 13, 1988, 133-51: 'an utopian tactical treatise' (151); M.Weinfeld, *The Organizational Pattern and the Penal Code of the Qumran Sect. A Comparison with Guilds and Religious Associations of the Hellenistic-Roman Period*, NTOA 2, Fribourg CH and Göttingen 1986.

251. Cf. also M.Philonenko, 'La Parabole sur la lampe (Luc 11, 33-36) et les horoscopes qoumraniens', *ZNW* 79, 1988, 145-51; id., 'Philon d'Alexandrie et l'"Instruction sur les deux Esprits"', in *Hellenica et Judaica. Hommage à V.Nikiprowetzky*, ed. A.Caquot, M.Hadas-Lebel and J.Riaud, Louvain and Paris 1986, 61-8.

252. Hengel, *Judaism and Hellenism* (n.16), index s.v. Astrology (II, 296); W. and H.G.Gundel, *Astrologumena*, Sudhoffs Archiv Beiheft 6, 1966; J.H. Charlesworth, 'Jewish Astrology in the Talmud, Pseudepigrapha, in the Dead Sea Scrolls and Early Palestine Synagogues', *HTR* 70, 1977, 183-200; M.Smith, 'Helios in Palestine', *ErIs* 16, 1982, 199-214.

253. Hengel, 'Rabbinische Legende' (n.110), 19 and n.23. There is an urgent need for a comprehensive account of Jewish magic in antiquity. W.Fauth, 'Arbath Iao. Zur mystischen Vierheit in griechischen und koptischen Zaubertexten und in gnostischen und apokryphen Schriften des christlichen Orients', *OrChr* 67, 1983, 65-103, shows the degree to which Old Testament formulae and terms sometimes in Hebrew have influenced the magical papyri and Gnostic texts.

254. J.H.Charlesworth, M.Hengel, D.Mendels, 'The Polemical Character of "On Kingship" in the Temple Scroll: An Attempt at Dating 11Q Temple', *JJS* 37, 1986, 23-38.

255. Thus e.g. E.Zeller, *Grundriss der Geschichte der griechischen Philosophie*, Leipzig 1893, 275-7, and id., *Philosophie der Griechen in ihrer geschichtlichen Entwicklung*, ed. F.Lortzing, W.Nestle and E.Wellmann, Vol.3/2, Leipzig ⁵1923 (reprinted Hildesheim 1964), 307-77, esp.365ff.

256. δύο τρίβους, Sirach 2.12; cf. TestAsh 1.3,5 δύο διαβούλια; cf. my *Judaism and Hellenism* (n.16), I, 140 and II, 91 n.224; T.Middendorp, *Die Stellung Jesu ben Siras zwischen Judentum und Hellenismus*, Leiden 1973 (also my review in *JSJ* 5, 1974, 83-87); M.Küchler, *Frühjüdische Weisheitstraditionen. Zum Fortgang weisheitlichen Denkens im Bereich des frühjüdischen Jahweglaubens*, OBO 26, Fribourg CH and Göttingen 1979; J.Marböck, *Sir 38,24-39,11: Der schriftgelehrte Weise. Ein Beitrag zu Gestalt und Werk Ben Siras*, BETL 51, Louvain 1979; R.Pautrel, 'Ben Sira et le Stoicisme', *RSR* 51, 1963, 535-49; O.Rickenbacher, *Weisheitsperikopen bei Ben Sira*, OBO 1, Fribourg CH and Göttingen 1973; J.T.Sanders, *Ben Sira and Demotic Wisdom*, SBL Monograph Series 27, Chico, CA 1983; further literature in Schürer, *History* III (n.25), 208-12.

257. Xenophon, *Mem.* 2.1.21-34: see Persius, *Sat.* 3.56f. on Y as the symbol of the two ways: 'the letter too which spreads out into the Samian branches'.

258. Urbach, *The Sages* (n.207) 1,471-83 (VI. The Two Inclinations'); cf. also 1QS 3,18-22 (Hengel, 'Qumran und der Hellenismus' [n.100], 355).

259. P. von der Osten-Sacken, *Gott und Belial. Traditionsgeschichtliche Untersuchungen zum Dualismus in den Texten von Qumran*, SUNT 6, Göttingen 1969; R.Stegemann, 'Zum Textbestand und Grundgedanken von 1 QS III,13-IV,26', *RdQ* 13, 1988, 95-131; however, the interpretation in terms of history of religion is inadequate.

260. Josephus, *BJ* 2.162: the Pharisees attribute everything to εἱμαρμένη; the Sadducees reject this conception (2.162): human beings have freedom of will (ἐκλογή, ibid., 165); cf. G.Maier, *Mensch und freier Wille. Nach den jüdischen Religionsparteien zwischen Ben Sira und Paulus*, WUNT 12, Tübingen 1971.

261. Cf. my Excursus 4 ' "Higher Wisdom through Revelation" as a Characteristic of Religion in Late Antiquity', in *Judaism and Hellenism* (n.16) I, 210-17.

262. Although the Greeks too could call on God as Father, as is shown for example by the Zeus hymn of the Stoic Cleanthes (*SVF* I, 537, 131-3, German translation in M.Pohlenz, *Die Stoa. Geschichte einer geistige Bewegung* I, Göttingen ⁴1970, 109f.; cf. id., 'Cleanthes' Zeushymnus', in id., *Kleine Schriften* I, ed. H.Dörrie, Hildesheim 1965, 87-93). See G.Schrenk, πατήρ, *TDNT* V, Grand Rapids 1967, 946-59.

263. A.von Harnack, *What is Christianity?* (1900), ET reissued New York 1957, 51. For the issue see my *Nachfolge und Charisma* (n.161), 31-40 and A.D.Nock, 'Bekehrung', *RAC* 2, Stuttgart 1954, 105-18; id., *Conversion. The Old and the New in Religion from Alexander the Great to Augustine of Hippo*, Oxford 1933.

264. Harnack, *What is Christianity?* (n.263), 33.

265. 'This notion of the *particular man* (my italics) before God speculative theology never gets into its head, it can only universalize the particular man fantastically' (S.Kierkegaard, *The Sickness unto Death*, Princeton and London 1941, 133).

266. Ps.44 (43).23 is not praise of the martyrs but an accusation against God; cf. Ps.69 (68).8. At most we find echoes in the archaic song of Deborah, Judg.5.18, and the Gideon tradition in Judg.9.17; cf. also I Sam.19.5; Judg.12.3 – i.e. relatively old traditions. Isa.53 is a unique, enigmatic special instance. For the whole question see my *The Atonement* (n.6), in *The Cross of the Son of God* (n.6), 104-206.

267. N.Brox, *Zeuge und Märtyrer. Untersuchungen zur frühchristlichen Zeugnis-Terminologie*, SANT 5, Munich 1961, 144-60; J.Jeremias, *New Testament Theology*, Vol.1, *The Proclamation of Jesus*, London and New York 1971, 292ff.; id., 'Das Lösegeld für Viele', first published in *Jud.* 3, 1947-8, 249-64, in id., *Abba*, Göttingen 1966, 216-29; E.Lohse, *Märtyrer und Gottesknecht*, FRLANT 64, Göttingen ²1963, 9-110.

268. Cf. Hengel, *Atonement* (n.6), 198f.; cf. also the survey of scholarship in Brox, *Zeuge und Märtyrer* (n.267), 132-42.

269. *'Quid Athenis et Hierosolymis?* Bemerkungen über die Herkunft von Aspekten des "Effective Death"'', in *Die Entstehung der jüdischen Martyrologie*, ed. J.W.van Henten, StPB 38, 1989, with numerous other valuable contributions on the theme.

270. R.Meyer, *Hellenistisches in der rabbinischen Anthropologie. Rabbinische Vorstellungen vom Werden des Menschen*, BWANT 74, Stuttgart 1937.

271. S.Lieberman, 'How Much Greek in Jewish Palestine?', first published in *Biblical and Other Studies*, ed. A.Altmann, LIAJS, Texts and Studies 1, Cambridge 1963, 123-41; now in *Essays in Greco-Roman and Related Talmudic Literature*, selected with a Prolegomenon by H.A.Fischel, LBS, New York 1977, 325-43, or in S.Lieberman, *Texts and Studies*, New York 1976, 216-34; id., *Hellenism in Jewish Palestine* (n.177); *Greek in Jewish Palestine. Studies in the Life and Manners of Jewish Palestine in the II-IV Centuries CE*, New York ²1965; cf. also S.R.Shimoff, 'Hellenization among the Rabbis: Some Evidence from Early Aggadot concerning David and Solomon', *JSJ* 18, 1987, 168-87.

272. See the note above; also id., *Rabbinic Literature and Greco-Roman Philosophy. A Study of Epicurea and Rhetorica in Early Midrashic Writings*, StPB 21, Leiden 1973.

273. S.Krauss, *Griechische und lateinische Lehnwörter* (n.28). Of course there are more recent introductory works; see those mentioned in n.28 above.

274. D.Daube, 'Alexandrian Methods of Interpretation and the Rabbis', first published in FS H.Lewald, Basel 1953, 27-44; reprinted in *Essays* (n.271), 165-82; or id., 'Rabbinic Methods of Interpretation and Hellenistic Rhetoric', *HUCA* 22, 1949, 239-64. For this subject see also S.R.Shimoff, 'Hellenization' (n.270), 168-87. H.L.Strack and G.Stemberger, *Einleitung in Talmud und Midrasch*, Munich ⁷1982, 26f., also mention further literature.

275. G.Mayer, 'Exegese II (Judentum)', *RAC* 6, Stuttgart 1966, 1194-1211.

276. mJad.4.6, *spry hmyrs*, cf. my *Judaism and Hellenism* (n.16) I, 66f., and index s.v. Homer, 310; also 'Achilleus in Jerusalem. Eine spätantike Messingkanne mit Achilleus-Darstellungen aus Jerusalem', in collaboration with R.Peled, SHAW.PH 1, 1982, 51.

277. mBik 1.5 etc.; cf. S.Krauss, *Griechische und Lateinische Lehnwörter* (n.28), II (1899), 64f., 598; R.Meyer, *Hellenistisches in der rabbinischen Anthropologie* (n.270), 68 (GenR 8 §1, ed. J.Theodor and C.Albeck, 55), and G.Kittel, *Probleme des palästinischen Spätjudentums* (n.4), 142-68, on the conception of the 'wheel of creation (or time)' (*glgl hw' shwzrb'wlm*; W.Jaeger, *Early Christianity* [n.21], 8, differs), a motif which really comes from the context of the discussion of the migration of souls. The appearance of this theme in the Hellenistic sphere has been investigated by M.Dibelius, *Der Brief des Jakobus*, KEK 15, with additions by H.Greeven and F.Hahn, Göttingen [12]1984, 182-4; for the subject see of course still E.Norden, *P. Vergilius Maro. Aeneis Buch VI*, Leipzig 1903, 16-19, on the τόπος περὶ παλιγγενεσίας in Virgil, *Aeneid* VI, 723-55, v.748: *ubi mille rotam volvere per annos*.

278. Lieberman, *Greek in Jewish Palestine* (n.270), 144-60 ('Greek and Latin Proverbs in the Rabbinic Literature'). For motifs from Greek mythology see (Strack) Billerbeck IV, 405f., 408ff.

279. Cf. J.Neusner, 'Die Suche nach dem historischen Hillel', in id., *Das pharisäische und talmudische Judentum. Neue Wege zu seinem Verständnis*, TSAJ 4, Tübingen 1984, 52-73, and N.N.Glatzer, *Hillel. Repräsentant des klassischen Judentums*, Bibliotheka Judaica, Frankfurt am Main 1966.

280. J.Jeremias, 'Goldene Regel 2', in *RGG³* 2, Tübingen 1958, 1688f.; A.Dihle, *Die goldene Regel. Eine Einführung in die Geschichte der antiken und frühchristlichen Vulgärethik*, SAW 7, Göttingen 1962, 82; Hengel, 'Zur matthäischen Bergpredigt' (n.137), 390-5, with instances from the rabbinic literature and Near Eastern sources.

281. Urbach, *The Sages* (n.207), 243-54.

282. Hillel: Prosbolē mShebi 9.3; bGit 36b; mAb 1.12, 'Be of the disciples of Aaron, loving peace and pursuing peace (Ps.34.15; Isa.51.1 and the διώκειν εἰρήνην in Heb.12.14: *rwdp šlwm*), loving mankind and bringing them nigh to the Law' (Danby [ed.], *The Mishnah* [n.163]: for a translation see Urbach, *The Sages* [n.207] 1, 588, and Glatzer, *Hillel* [n.278], 75-80).

283. H.D.Betz, *Der Apostel Paulus und die sokratische Tradition. Eine exegetische Untersuchung zu seiner 'Apologie' II Korinther 10-13*, BHT 45, Tübingen 1972, 138-48.

284. F.Büchsel, *Johannes und der hellenistische Synkretismus*, BFCT 2.R.16, Gütersloh 1928, 53.

285. I can only wonder at the self-confidence with which many of my New Testament colleagues talk about '*the* Gnostic myth' or 'Gnosticism' in the singular. This myth, as described, say by Bultmann in numerous publications (*Theology of the New Testament* [n.4] 1, 172-4; *Primitive Christianity* [n.4], 162-74) *before* the discovery of the Nag Hammadi texts (and the discussion about Gnosticism which was considerably changed by them) is an ahistorical construction of the history-of-religions school, as C.Colpe has aptly made

clear (id., *Die religionsgeschichtliche Schule. Darstellung und Kritik ihres Bildes vom gnostischen Erlösermythos*, FRLANT 78, Göttingen 1961). Already eleven years before Colpe's book, a great expert in the history of Hellenistic religion, A.D.Nock, had made an energetic protest backed up with sources in his review of Bultmann's *Primitive Christianity* (NSNU 5, 1951, 35-40). But this was completely passed over in Germany. Certainly Bultmann, who here took over the findings of his generation of teachers, had sometimes spoken of 'manifold variations' (*Primitive Christianity*, 156), but when he had done so it was always in the interest of the theological *systematization* of the disparate evidence; he falsely unified the evidence and drew misleading *historical* consequences from it. His question about the 'understanding of human nature' (ibid., 166) in John, Paul or Gnostic authors is certainly legitimate in the preoccupation of a theologian with this phenomenon, even if regrets must be expressed at a number of blurred features in the picture which is thus arrived at, and the separation between contemporary understanding of existence in the present and the historical understanding gained from the text is not always successful. But in the process, above all the ahistorical construction of '*the* Gnostic myth' which in some way is supposed to underlie New Testament texts – sometimes as an antithesis – all too easily leads to caricatures. At the same time the philosophical premise of timeless existentialia as a general feature which first enables understanding in each individual instance emerges in a negative way. In his article 'The Problem of Hermeneutics' (1950) in *Essays Philosophical and Theological*, London 1955, 234-61, Bultmann makes this more precise in the context of the various 'life-relationships' of the text and exegetes whose relationship, following Dilthey, he regarded as the 'presupposition of every proper interpretation' (236). However, a false *historical* ordering of the 'life-relationships' which are expressed in a text carries with it the danger that these too cannot be precisely arrived at and depicted. The great work by Hans Jonas (*Gnosis und spätantiker Geist*, I, *Die mythologische Gnosis*, Göttingen ²1954, which the author himself considerably corrected at the 1966 Messina Congress, see *Gnosis und Gnostizismus*, WdF 262, ed. K.Rudolph, Darmstadt 1975, 626-45) certainly shows how for all the problems of individual results and his concept of Gnosticism, which is drawn too wide, the leading question of the *nature* of the phenomenon which is the topic here is often a decisive help in the individual analysis of Gnostic systems and themes. The decisive point in the dispute as to whether earlier primitive Christianity is dependent on a 'pre-Christian Gnosticism' which *cannot be demonstrated* in the sources is not answered here in any way. Of course to a large degree it is also a problem of definition: the wider the concept of Gnosticism is made, the more texts can be subsumed under it. But such an extension certainly does not further the understanding of the texts in their irreplacable particularity. In a way for which we should be grateful, Colpe has made it clear that underlying the 'Gnostic Redeemer myth' of the history of religions school and its disciples was '*de facto* the Manichaean system, which as the result of an unfortunate combination of circumstances in the scholarly world had been put forward at that time by Near Eastern scholars' (C.Colpe,

'Mythische und religiöse Aussage ausserhalb und innerhalb des Christentums', in id., *Theologie, Ideologie, Religionswissenschaft. Demonstration ihrer Unterscheidung*, TB 68, Munich 1980, 101). I must leave to the reader to decide whether Colpe's interpretation of this historical mistake on the part of existential interpretation with the help of a brilliantly malicious comment by Karl Kraus about psychoanalysis really describes the genesis or even the motive of Bultmann's views. But in considering German research into Gnosticism from Reitzenstein via the Marburg school to its present descendants, one has already to say *difficile est saturam non scribere*.

286. Sextus Julius Africanus, *Ep.ad Aristidem* 5 (ed.W.Reichardt, TU 34.3, Leipzig 1909, 61 line 20, or PG 10, 61.14). Julius Africanus himself already gives Jerusalem as place of birth; see most recently F.C.R.Thee, *Julius Africanus and the Early Christian View of Magic*, HUTh 19, Tübingen 1984.

287. E.Norden, *Die antike Kunstprosa vom VI. Jahrhundert vor Christus bis in die Zeit der Renaissance*, Vol.2, Leipzig and Berlin 1909, 451-510.

288. Cf. the interpretation which W.Jaeger gives in *Early Christianity* (n.21), 12-26. Jaeger points to the use of 'rhetorical precepts' (ibid., 10), to borrowing from Stoic philosophy (14), and examples from political life (19).

289. Cf. M.Hengel, 'Hadrians Politik gegenüber Juden und Christen', in *JANES* 16/17, 1987 (*Ancient Studies in Memory of E.Bickerman*), 153-82: 161f., and for Justin, H.Chadwick, 'The Vindication of Christianity' (1966), in *Early Christian Thought and the Classical Tradition. Studies in Justin, Clement and Origen*, Oxford 1984, 1-30; Chadwick also describes a shift when he rejects connections between Justin's theology of the Logos and the concept of the Logos in John (ibid., 4) and stresses the significance of Hellenistic popular philosophy for Justin (ibid., 11-13); see also Jaeger, *Early Christianity* (n.21), 26-30.E.Schwartz endorsed the fact that Papias, so severly chided by Eusebius, 'had a command of the art of rhetoric' ('Über den Tod der Söhne Zebedäi. Ein Beitrag zur Geschichte des Johannesevangeliums', first published in *AGWG.PH* 7/5, 1904, and then in id., *Gesammelte Schriften* 5, *Zum Neuen Testament und zum frühen Christentum*, Berlin 1965, 48-123, and in *Johannes und sein Evangelium*, ed. K.H.Rengstorf, WdF 82, Darmstadt 1973, 202-90: 211) and writes too well for 'mere simplicity' (ibid., 216).

290. Jaeger, *Early Christianity* (n.21), 11f. Here Jaeger also cites a passage from the Acts of Philip related to Acts 17.17-34, according to which Philip disputes in Athens with 300 philosophers who took him to be a philosopher by his clothing (Acts of Philip 6 [1], ed. R.A.Lipsius and M.Bonnet, 2/2,4) and says there: 'Καὶ γὰρ παιδείαν ὄντως νέαν καὶ καινὴν ἤνεγκεν ὁ κύριός μου εἰς τὸν κόσμον' (Acts of Philip 8[3], Lipsius/Bonnet, 5). The term *paideia* betrays the degree of Hellenization of the kerygma in this text, though it is evidently late.

291. A.von Harnack, *History of Dogma* 1 ([3]1900), reissued New York and London 1961, 226; cf. also the description of the background of Ritschlian theology and a sophisticated judgment in W.Pannenberg, 'The Appropriation of the Philosophical Concept of God as a Dogmatic Problem of Early Christian Theology' (1959), in id., *Basic Questions in Theology* 2, London and Philadelphia

1971, 119-83, and now E.P.Meijering, *Die Hellenisierung des Christentums im Urteil A.v.Harnacks*, Transactions of the Koniklijke Nederlandse Akademie van Wetenschappen, Afd.Letterkunde, Nieuwe Reeks, 128, 1987. However, Harnack's concept of Hellenism is essentially different from that which is usually presupposed nowadays. He understood the most important sign of 'Hellenism' to be a form of 'academic' education not only in the sphere of rhetoric but above all in the realm of philosophy. If we use this concept as a basis, the 'Hellenization' of Christianity is beginning only now, as in fact the philosophical and rhetorical level of Hellenism which the Jew Philo and others had long taken for granted was arrived at in the early church relatively late and gradually with Justin, or even better with Clement of Alexandria.

Abbreviations

CorpAp	*Corpus Apologetorum*
CP	*Classical Philology*
CPJ	*Corpus papyrorum Judaicorum*
CQ	*Classical Quarterly*
CRB	Cahiers de la Revue Biblique
CUFr	Collection des Universités de France
DBS	*Dictionnaire de la Bible, Supplément*
DJD	Discoveries in the Judaean Desert
EJ	*Encyclopaedia Judaica*
EKK	Evangelisch-katholischer Kommentar zum Neuen Testament
EPRO	Etudes préliminaires aux religions orientales dans l'empire romain
ErIs	*Eretz Israel*
ET	English translation
EvTh	*Evangelische Theologie*
ExpT	*Expository Times*
FChLDG	Forschungen zur christlichen Literatur– und Dogmengeschichte
FGrHist	*Fragmente der griechischen Historiker*
FRLANT	Forschungen zur Religion des Alten und Neuen Testaments
FS	*Festschrift*
GCS	Die Griechischen Christlichen Schriftsteller der ersten drei Jahrhunderte
GLAJ	*Greek and Latin Authors on Jews and Judaism*, ed. M. Stern
GOF.H	Göttinger Forschungen. Historische Abteilung
HAW	Handbuch der Altertumswissenschaft
HNT	Handbuch zum Neuen Testament
HUCA	*The Hebrew Union College Annual*
HuTh	Hermeneutische Untersuchungen zur Theologie
IEJ	*Israel Exploration Journal*
JANES	*Journal of the Ancient Near Eastern Society*, Columbia University
JBL.MS	Journal of Biblical Literature. Monograph Series
JE	*Jewish Encyclopedia*
JJS	*Journal of Jewish Studies*
JQR	*Jewish Quarterly Review*
JSHRZ	Jüdische Schriften aus hellenistisch-römischer Zeit
JSOT.MS	Journal for the Study of the Old Testament. Monograph Series
JSJ	*Journal for the Study of Judaism*
JSS	*Journal of Semitic Studies*

KEK	Kritisch-exegetisches Kommentar über das Neue Testament
KP	*Kleine Pauly*
LBS	Library of Biblical Studies
LCL	Loeb Classical Library
LIAJS	Lown Institute of Advanced Judaic Studies
LXX	Septuagint
NF (NS)	Neue Folge (New Series)
NHS	Nag Hammadi Studies
NSNU	*Nuntius sodalicii neotestamentici Upsaliensis*
NT.S	Novum Testamentum. Supplements
NTA	Neutestamentliche Abhandlungen
NTOA	Novum Testamentum et Orbis Antiquus
NTS	*New Testament Studies*
NT.S	*Novum Testament* Supplements
NumC	*Numismatic Chronicle and Journal of the Numismatic Society*
OBO	Orbis Biblicus et Orientalis
OGIS	W. Dittenberger, *Orientis Graeci Inscriptiones Selectae*
OrChr	*Oriens Christianus*
OTS	Old Testament Studies
PCPS	*Proceedings of the Cambridge Philological Society*
PEQ	*Palestine Exploration Quarterly*
PG	J. P. Migne, *Patrologia Graeca*
PRE	*Paulys Real-Encyclopädie der classischen Altertumswissenschaft*
PSVTGr	Pseudepigrapha Veteris Testamenti Graeca
PW	*Paulys Real-Encyclopädie der classischen Alterthumswissenschaft*
Qad.	*Qadmoniot*
R	Reihe (Series)
RAC	*Reallexikon für Antike und Christentum*
RB	*Revue biblique*
RdQ	*Revue de Qumran*
RGG	*Die Religion in Geschichte und Gegenwart*
RHPR	*Revue d'histoire et philosophie religieuses*
RM	Religionen der Menschheit
RSR	*Revue des sciences religieuuses*
SANT	Studien zum Alten und Neuen Testament
SAW	Studienhefte zur Altertumswissenschaft
SBF.CMa	Studium biblicum Franciscanum – Collectio major
SBL	Society of Biblical Literature
SBT	Studies in Biblical Theology
SBW	Studien der Bibliothek Warburg

SEG	*Supplementum Epigraphicum Graecum*
SGU	*Studia Graeca Upsaliensia*
SHAW.PH	Sitzungsberichte der Heidelberger Akademie der Wissenschaften, philosophisch-historische Klasse
SJ	Studia Judaica
SJLA	Studies in Jewish Life in Antiquity
SSA	Schriften der Sektion für Altertumswissenschaft
StNT	Studien zum Neuen Testament
StPB	Studia post-biblica
SUNT	Studien zur Umwelt des Neuen Testaments
SVF	Stoicorum Veterum Fragmenta
SVTP	Studia in veteris testamenti pseudepigrapha
TaS	Texts and Studies
TB	Theologische Bücherei
TDNT	*Theological Dictionary of the New Testament*, ed. G. Kittel
ThBeitr	*Theologische Beiträge*
ThQ	*Theologische Quartalschrift*
ThR	*Theologische Revue*
TLZ	*Theologische Literaturzeitung*
TRE	*Theologische Realenzyklopädie*
TSAJ	Texte und Studien zum Antiken Judentum
TSJTSA	Texts and Studies of the Jewish Theological Seminary of America
TU	Texte und Untersuchungen
TW	Theologische Wissenschaft
UB	Urban-Bücher
UCPH	University of California Publications in History
VF	*Verkündigung und Forschung*
WdF	Wege der Forschung
WUNT	Wissenschaftliche Untersuchungen zum Neuen Testament
ZAW	*Zeitschrift für die alttestamentliche Wissenschaft*
ZDPV	*Zeitschrift des deutschen Palästinavereins*
ZKG	*Zeitschrift für Kirchengeschichte*
ZNW	*Zeitschrift für die neutestamentliche Wissenschaft*
ZPE	*Zeitschrift für Papyrologie und Epigraphik*
ZSTh	*Zeitschrift für Systematische Theologie*
ZTK	*Zeitschrift für Theologie und Kirche*

Index of Modern Scholars

Index of Names and Places from Antiquity